The Burj Khalifa, the tallest building in the world, soars into the sky in Dubai, United Arab Emirates.

The northern lights shimmer in the sky above Iceland.

LITTLE KIDS FIRST BIG BOOK OF WHERE

JILL ESBAUM

NATIONAL GEOGRAPHIC KiDS

WASHINGTON, D.C.

A huge sculpture of a hand rises from the Atacama Desert in Chile.

CONTENTS

Introduction 6
How to Use This Book 7
Map of the World 8

CHAPTER 1
WHERE CAN I SEE THAT? 10
Where Is Earth's Biggest Ocean? 12
Where Is the World's Highest Mountain? 14
Where Is the Deepest Spot on the Planet? 16
Where Are the Most Volcanoes? 18
Where Is the Biggest Cave? 20
Where Is Earth's Largest Rainforest? 22
Where Is the Biggest Rock on Earth? 24
Where Is the Biggest Glacier? 26
Try This! 27
Where Is Earth's Biggest Desert? 28
Where Is the Longest River? 30
Where Is the World's Biggest Waterfall? 32
Where Can I See the Most Stars? 34
Map Fun! 36

CHAPTER 2
ANIMALS EVERYWHERE 38
Where Is the World's Biggest Animal? 40
Where Do the Biggest Snakes Live? 42
Where Are the Loudest Animals? 44
Where Does the Loudest Insect Live? 46
Try This! 47
Where Do Koalas Live? 48
Where Is Home for Giant Pandas? 50
Where Do Fish Go When Lakes and Rivers Freeze? 52
Where Do Birds Sleep? 54
Where Do Animals Migrate? 56
Where Did People First Have Pets? 60
Where Do Arctic Animals Go to Keep Warm? 62
Try This! 63
Where Do Penguins Live? 64

Where Do Animals Live in Antarctica? 66
Where Are Wild Monkeys Found? 68
Where Do Real Dragons Live? 70
Where Did *Tyrannosaurus Rex* Roam? 72
Map Fun! 74

CHAPTER 3
WHERE DID THAT COME FROM? 76
Where Was Pizza Invented? 78
Where Were the First Books Made? 82
Where Are TV Shows Made? 84
Where Were Bicycles Invented? 86
Where Were Board Games Invented? 90
Where Does the Water Go When I Flush? 92
Where Does Our Garbage Go? 94
Map Fun! 96

CHAPTER 4
WHERE CAN I FIND THAT? 98
Where Is the Biggest Sports Stadium? 100
Where Is the World's Tallest Building? 102
Where Are the Most Mysterious Places? 106
Where Are the World's Twistiest Roads? 108
Where Is the World's Highest Bridge? 110
Where Is the Tallest Ferris Wheel? 112
Where Are the Coolest Theme Parks? 114
Where Is the Most Fun Place to Live? 118
Try This! 119
Map Fun! 120

Parent Tips 122
Glossary 124
Additional Resources 125
Index 126
Photo Credits 127
Acknowledgments 128

INTRODUCTION

This book takes curious readers to some of the most amazing places our world has to offer. It answers questions from "Where is the world's highest mountain?" and "Where can I see the most stars?" to "Where is the world's biggest animal?" and "Where was pizza invented?"

On pages 8 and 9, you will see examples of world maps that show the shapes, locations, and features of Earth's seven major landmasses, or continents. You can use them to help find the places mentioned in the chapters that follow, which are sprinkled with more maps. These maps help pinpoint all kinds of interesting locations, from volcano-packed regions to penguin-packed areas. Filled with fascinating facts about natural wonders, human-made wonders, animals, and more, this book can be read from cover to cover or dipped into one page at a time.

CHAPTER ONE explores Earth's extremes and other natural wonders—the largest cave, the deepest spot on the planet, the biggest rainforest, the longest river, and more.

CHAPTER TWO journeys around the planet to discover some of Earth's most impressive animals, from the loudest insect to the biggest snake. Readers also find out where birds sleep, where fish go when water freezes, and other intriguing facts about animal behavior.

CHAPTER THREE shows readers where some of their favorite things were invented, from pizza to ice cream, from books to skateboards and more. Kids also learn where some things go, such as where the water goes when we flush.

CHAPTER FOUR takes readers to some of the world's most famous and fun human-made places. Marvel over the tallest building, mysterious monuments, and the coolest theme parks ever.

HOW TO USE THIS BOOK

COLORFUL PHOTOGRAPHS illustrate each spread, supporting the text and showcasing a wide variety of interesting places.

POP-UP FACTS sprinkled throughout provide added information and build on the main text in each section.

INTERACTIVE QUESTIONS in each section encourage conversation related to the topics.

A map-themed **ACTIVITY** at the end of each chapter reinforces concepts covered in that section.

In the back of the book, find **MORE FOR PARENTS,** including tips such as fun geography-related activities, additional resources, and a helpful glossary.

7

MAP OF THE WORLD

Maps tell you what a place is like, even if you've never been there. For example, a black solid line can mean the boundary between countries. A black dot usually stands for a city. If you don't know what a symbol on a map means, check the map key.

POLITICAL MAP

There are two main types of maps. Political maps show the outlines of countries. They can also mark the location of cities and capitals. Physical maps are the second type of map. These maps show an area's land and water features. You can see the locations of mountain ranges, forests, deserts, plains, and bodies of water such as lakes, rivers, and oceans.

PHYSICAL MAP

Explorers camp near the entrance to the world's largest cave, Hang Son Doong in Vietnam.

CHAPTER 1
WHERE CAN I SEE THAT?

Our Earth is an extraordinary planet. Its ocean, land, and sky are filled with natural and human-made wonders that will amaze and astonish you.

WHERE IS EARTH'S BIGGEST OCEAN?

Most of our planet is covered by one big ocean! But different parts of this ocean have been given names: Pacific Ocean, Atlantic Ocean, Indian Ocean, and Arctic Ocean. All these parts of Earth's ocean are connected.

EARTH looks **BLUE** from **SPACE** because the **OCEAN COVERS** about three-quarters of it.

NATURAL WONDERS

CORAL REEF

Oceans are also home to **CORAL REEFS,** which are made up of layers of the **SKELETONS** from tiny animals called **POLYPS.** The **GREAT BARRIER REEF** in Australia is Earth's biggest coral reef.

POLYPS

The biggest part is the Pacific Ocean. The Atlantic Ocean is next biggest, then the Indian Ocean. The Arctic Ocean is the smallest of Earth's four oceans.

Most of the living things on Earth live in the ocean, from teeny creatures too small to see without a microscope to enormous whales.

Which ocean is nearest to your home?

WHERE IS THE WORLD'S HIGHEST MOUNTAIN?

The highest mountain on land is Mount Everest, part of the Himalayan mountain range in Asia. It rises more than five miles (8 km) above sea level!

Climbing Mount Everest takes months or years of planning and training. The mountain is rocky, icy, and steep. The weather can be dangerous, with sudden storms and freezing temperatures.

Where is the highest place you've climbed?

NATURAL WONDERS

Earth's longest mountain range is the Mid-Ocean Ridge. Most of it is underwater. It curves around the seven continents like a twisty snake.

MAP KEY — Mid-Ocean Ridge

MOUNT EVEREST

Local **SHERPA GUIDES** from Nepal often help climbers find the **BEST ROUTES** up Mount Everest.

THIN AIR at the top of Mount Everest makes it **HARDER TO BREATHE** the higher you get.

WHERE IS THE DEEPEST SPOT ON THE PLANET?

Off the coast of Asia, in the Pacific Ocean, there's a big groove in Earth's crust. This underwater groove is called the Mariana Trench.

A part of the trench called Challenger Deep is the deepest place on Earth. To get to the bottom of it, you would have to go nearly seven miles (11 km) straight down! That is too deep for people to explore with basic diving gear. So scientists travel in a submersible, a small vehicle made for underwater exploring.

This **SNAILFISH** is the **DEEPEST FISH** ever caught in the **MARIANA TRENCH.**

Sunlight from the surface can't reach the deepest parts of the ocean, so it is totally dark. A submersible has to shine plenty of light so explorers can see what is down there.

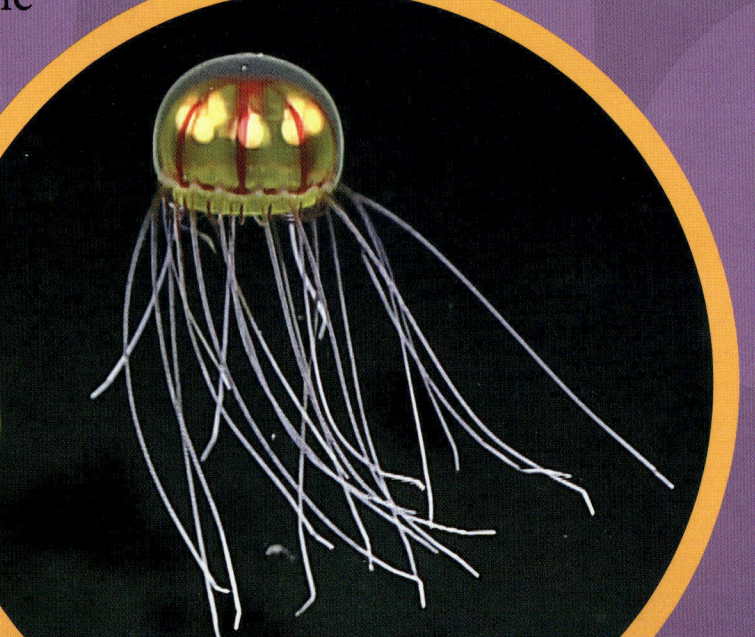

This **COOL JELLYFISH** was also found in the **MARIANA TRENCH.**

NATURAL WONDERS

To explore **DEEP PARTS OF THE OCEAN,** scientists travel in **SUBMERSIBLES** that are equipped with **POWERFUL LIGHTS.**

WHERE ARE THE MOST VOLCANOES?

Most of Earth's volcanoes are found around an area called the Ring of Fire in the Pacific Ocean. The Ring of Fire has more than 450 volcanoes. Many of them are hidden underwater.

Many of the **WORLD'S EARTHQUAKES** occur around the **RING OF FIRE.**

NATURAL WONDERS

ERUPTING VOLCANO

MOVING LAVA

A **SCIENTIST** who studies **VOLCANOES** is called a **VOLCANOLOGIST**.

VOLCANOLOGIST

Volcanoes can be active, dormant, or extinct. An active volcano is one that has erupted at least once in the past 10,000 years. A dormant volcano is not erupting, but is expected to at some point. An extinct volcano is one that has not erupted for at least 10,000 years, and scientists think it will not erupt again.

WHERE IS THE BIGGEST CAVE?

Hang Son Doong in Vietnam is the world's largest cave. Hang Son Doong is so big that the weather inside the cave is different from the weather outside. Clouds often hang near the cave's ceiling, which is so high that a 40-story building could fit inside.

Parts of Hang Son Doong's ceiling have fallen in. A jungle grows inside where beams of sunlight peek through. A river also flows through this enormous cave.

The world's longest cave system is Mammoth Cave in Kentucky, U.S.A. So far, more than 400 miles (644 km) of passages have been mapped.

What do you use to help you see in the dark?

MAMMOTH CAVE

HANG SON DOONG

NATURAL WONDERS

SAC ACTUN

The longest **UNDERWATER CAVE,** the Sac Actun, in **MEXICO,** has so many passages, it is like a **MAZE.**

WHERE IS EARTH'S LARGEST RAINFOREST?

South America's Amazon rainforest is the largest on Earth. It stretches through nine countries. Tropical rainforests grow in areas near Earth's Equator, where the temperature stays warm all year. In a rainforest, it rains nearly every day.

The Amazon rainforest is home to an incredible variety of animals. Many of them, like the animals shown here, are found nowhere else in the world.

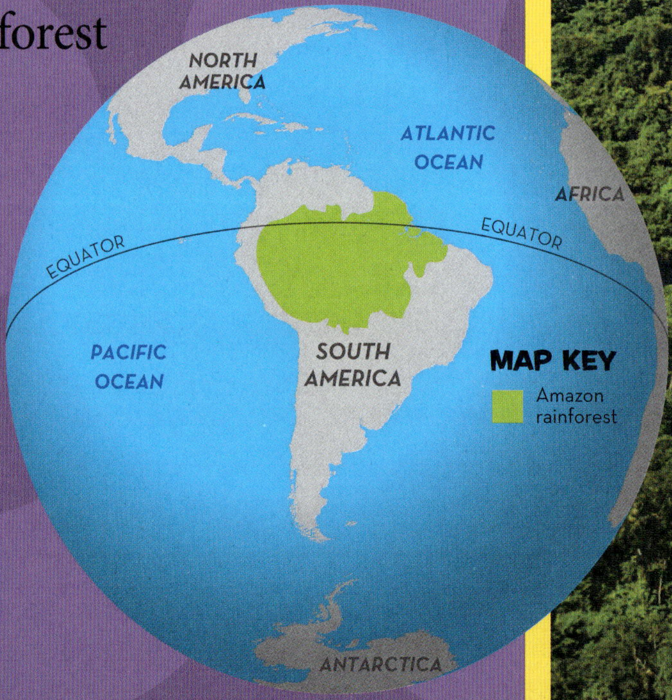

HOATZIN

AMAZON RAINFOREST

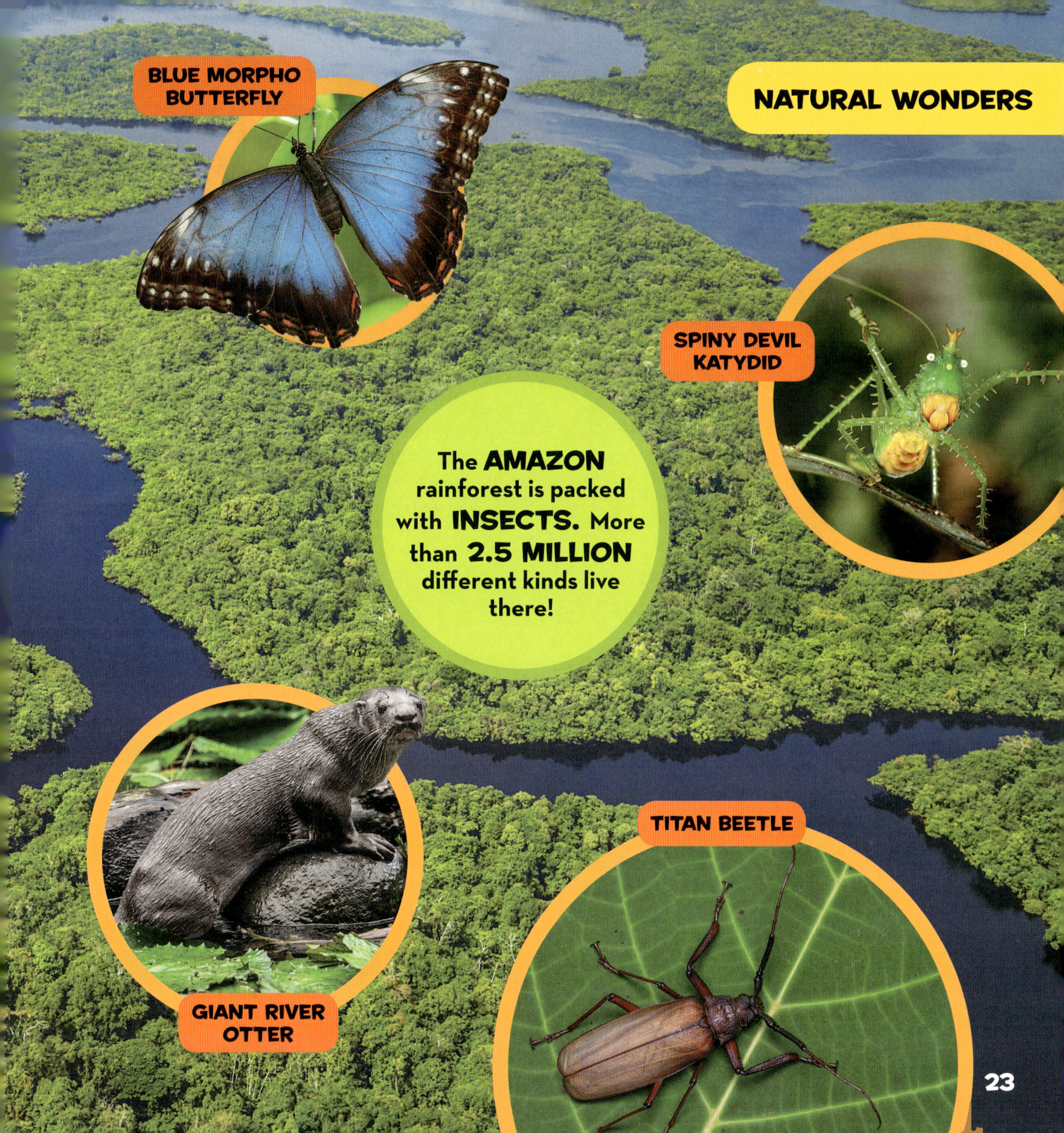

NATURAL WONDERS

BLUE MORPHO BUTTERFLY

SPINY DEVIL KATYDID

The **AMAZON** rainforest is packed with **INSECTS.** More than **2.5 MILLION** different kinds live there!

GIANT RIVER OTTER

TITAN BEETLE

WHERE IS THE BIGGEST ROCK ON EARTH?

In the middle of Australia is a big, dry, flat area called the outback. Right in the middle of the outback is the world's biggest single stone. The gigantic rock is called Uluru. To people native to the outback, Uluru is a sacred place. Visitors are asked to not climb it, but to walk around its base instead. Uluru is also known as Ayers Rock.

ULURU is more than **TWO MILES** (3 km) long. But what shows is **ONLY PART** of it. Most of it is **UNDERGROUND!**

NATURAL WONDERS

While Australia may be home to the biggest rock, you can find unusual rocks around the world. In Arches National Park, U.S.A., enormous rocks curve into gateways. The park has more than 2,000 of these stone arches.

ARCHES NATIONAL PARK

When **RAIN BEATS** against **SANDSTONE**, it wears away **TINY BITS OF ROCK.** Over thousands of years, that **CREATED THESE ARCHES.**

Have you ever found a rock with an unusual shape?

LAMBERT-FISHER GLACIER

WHERE IS THE BIGGEST GLACIER?

A glacier is a very slow-moving river of ice and snow. It moves so slowly that it looks like it is standing still. Antarctica's Lambert-Fisher Glacier is the biggest in the world.

Antarctica also has a red glacier! Because of its color, this glacier is called Blood Falls. It is red because of a mineral called iron in the water.

How slowly can you move?

BLOOD FALLS

TRY THIS! MELTING AWAY

YOU'LL NEED
3 small bowls
3 ice cubes
sugar
salt

Can you predict which ice cube will melt fastest?

1 Place an ice cube into each bowl and place the bowls in a row.

2 Sprinkle sugar on the first ice cube.

3 Sprinkle salt on the second ice cube.

4 Don't add anything to the third ice cube.

Which ice cube do you think will start melting first? Which ice cube do you think will stay frozen the longest? Leave the bowls on the counter for 20 minutes. Check the bowls. Were you right?

Water turns to ice at 32°F (0°C). Some things touch water and not much happens. But when salt touches water (or ice), it lowers that freezing point. That's why salt melts ice faster than sugar does.

WHERE IS EARTH'S BIGGEST DESERT?

If you think a desert has to be hot and sandy, think again! Deserts just have to be very, very dry, and no place on Earth is drier than Antarctica. Cold and icy Antarctica is the world's biggest desert.

A **DESERT** is a place that usually gets **FEWER THAN 10 INCHES** (25 cm) of **RAIN** or **SNOW** per year.

ANTARCTICA

Where is the coldest place you've been? Where is the hottest?

NATURAL WONDERS

Even the **SAHARA** can get **COLD AT NIGHT.** During part of the year, **NIGHTTIME** temperatures there drop **BELOW FREEZING.**

SAHARA DESERT

The Sahara, which covers parts of northern Africa, is the world's biggest hot desert. Many of the animals that live here, like the dromedary camel and the fennec fox, can go a long time without drinking any water.

The **DRIEST PLACE** in the world is a spot in Chile's **ATACAMA DESERT.** Almost **NO RAIN** falls here.

FENNEC FOX

ATACAMA DESERT

NILE RIVER

The **NILE** flows through **11 COUNTRIES** before reaching the **MEDITERRANEAN SEA.**

WHERE IS THE LONGEST RIVER?

Not all scientists agree on the answer to this question. It can be hard to measure the length of a river, because there are so many places where streams or other rivers join it.

NATURAL WONDERS

Some scientists think the Nile River, in Africa, is the longest in the world. Others believe that the Amazon River, in South America, is the longest.

There's one thing the experts all agree about: The Amazon River carries more water than any other river in the world.

AMAZON RIVER

The **AMAZON** River flows through **SIX COUNTRIES** before reaching the **ATLANTIC OCEAN**.

WHERE IS THE WORLD'S BIGGEST WATERFALL?

Waterfalls come in all shapes and sizes. The tallest waterfall is Angel Falls, in Venezuela, South America. The water falls so far—over half a mile (980 m)—that some of it turns into mist before even reaching the bottom.

ANGEL FALLS

NATURAL WONDERS

Which of these waterfalls would you most like to visit? Why?

KHONE FALLS

The widest waterfall in the world is Khone Falls, in Laos, Asia. This waterfall is 6.7 miles (11 km) wide, but it is not very high.

The cluster of stars called the **MILKY WAY** is made up of more than **200 BILLION STARS**—including our sun! We can only **SEE PARTS** of the Milky Way **FROM EARTH**.

WHERE CAN I SEE THE MOST STARS?

Most of the time, light helps us see. But when it comes to looking at the night sky, the best place to be is out in the country, far away from the glow of city lights. The darker the sky, the better. Look up. After your eyes adjust, little by little, stars will twinkle into view.

NATURAL WONDERS

AURORA BOREALIS

AURORA AUSTRALIS

Close to Earth's polar areas, you can sometimes see mysterious waves of color in the night sky. In the north, these lights are called *aurora borealis,* or northern lights. In the south, they are known as *aurora australis,* or southern lights. These awesome light shows happen when tiny particles from the sun smash into gases closer to our planet.

Where is your favorite place to look at stars?

MAP FUN!

This map shows where many of the amazing places you read about in Chapter One are located. With your finger, draw a line from each clue to the place it describes.

A. The biggest ocean

B. The highest mountain

C. The biggest hot desert

D. The biggest rock on earth

E. The widest waterfall

F. The driest place in the world

G. The biggest glacier

H. The largest rainforest

Which continent is your **HOME** on?

Which continent is **MOUNT EVEREST** found on?

CHAPTER 2
ANIMALS EVERYWHERE

Caribou travel together in Manitoba, Canada.

In this chapter, you will meet all kinds of animals, from big and loud to small and fierce. Let's find out what they are and where they live.

WHERE IS THE WORLD'S BIGGEST ANIMAL?

Dive into the ocean to meet the blue whale, Earth's largest animal. This giant mammal is twice as long as a tractor trailer!

A BLUE WHALE'S TONGUE weighs as much as an African **ELEPHANT.**

The **LARGEST LAND** animal is the **AFRICAN ELEPHANT.** Even the **EARS** of these elephants are **HUGE**—sometimes as big as a **BATHTUB.**

ANIMALS

The world's tallest animal, the giraffe, lives in Africa. Giraffes can be taller than a double-decker bus.

Africa is also home to the biggest bird, the ostrich. An ostrich is taller than your refrigerator.

Earth's biggest reptile is the saltwater crocodile. This meat-eater lives in parts of India, Asia, and Australia. It is longer than a small car.

This stick insect from China is the world's longest insect. It is longer than this open book!

What is the biggest animal you've ever seen?

WHERE DO THE BIGGEST SNAKES LIVE?

Do you like snakes? BIG snakes? Here are the places where they slither and slink.

The green anaconda is the world's *heaviest* snake. It weighs as much as an adult pig and is as big around as a watermelon. The anaconda lives in the rainforests of South America.

Southeast Asia is home to the world's longest constrictor snake, the reticulated python. This snake is about three times longer than your bed. Colorful patterns on this snake's skin make it hard to see on the ground.

ANACONDA

PYTHON

The python and anaconda are **CONSTRICTOR SNAKES.** They kill prey by **CURLING THEIR BODIES** around the animal and **SQUEEZING IT.**

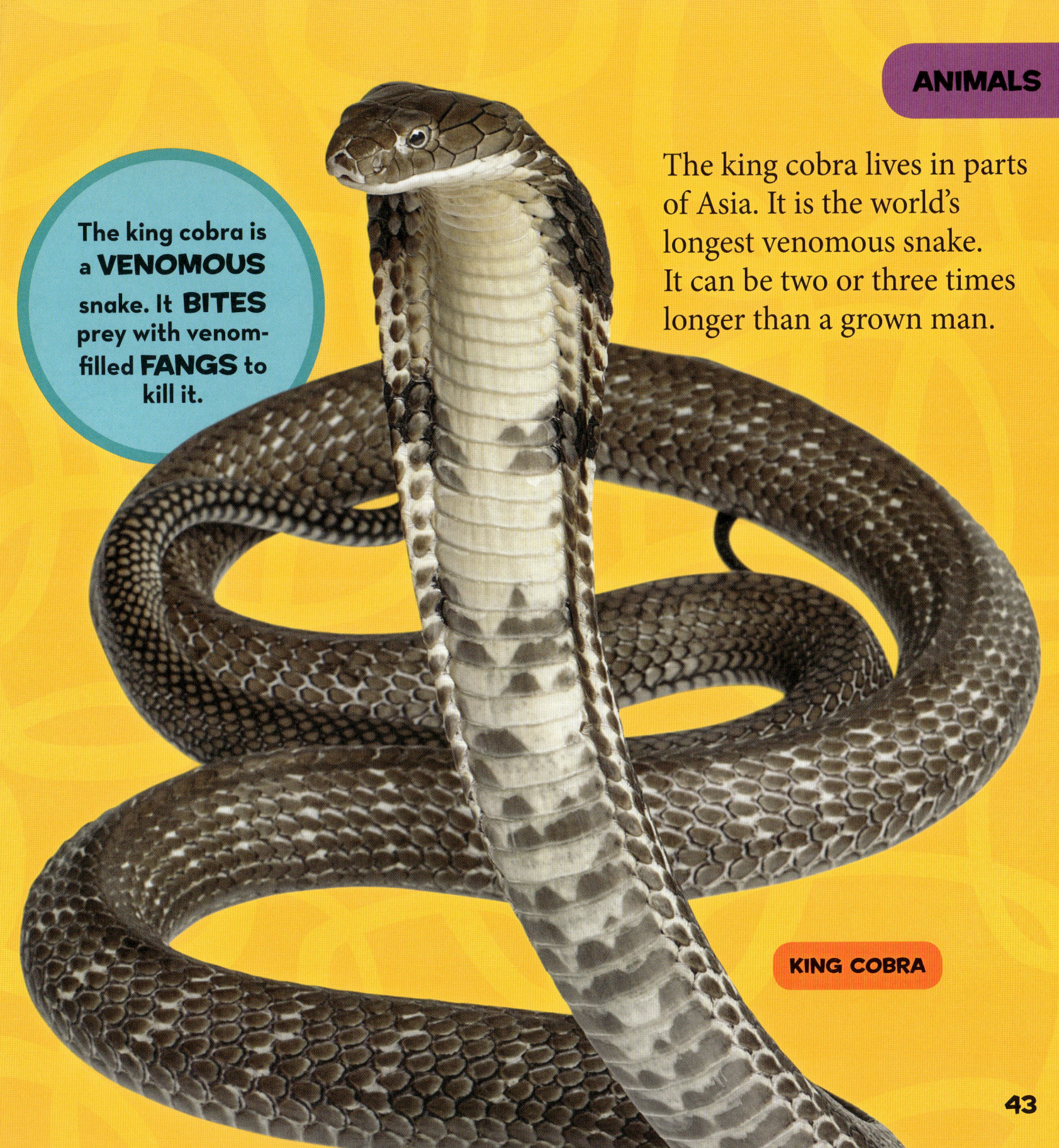

ANIMALS

The king cobra is a **VENOMOUS** snake. It **BITES** prey with venom-filled **FANGS** to kill it.

The king cobra lives in parts of Asia. It is the world's longest venomous snake. It can be two or three times longer than a grown man.

KING COBRA

WHERE ARE THE LOUDEST ANIMALS?

Some of Earth's loudest animals live in the ocean. Sperm whales are the loudest of all. These huge mammals make superloud knocking sounds called clicks.

Not all the noisy creatures in the ocean are big. The little snapping shrimp has a special claw that squirts out a bubble that hits and stuns prey. The bubble comes out so fast, it makes a loud cracking sound.

The African lion is one of the noisiest land animals. When it roars, its neighbors can hear the sound up to five miles (8 km) away!

The kakapo parrot, which lives on islands near New Zealand, has a squawk that can be heard as far as three miles (5 km) away.

A **LION'S ROAR** can be louder than a **MOTORCYCLE!**

AFRICAN LION

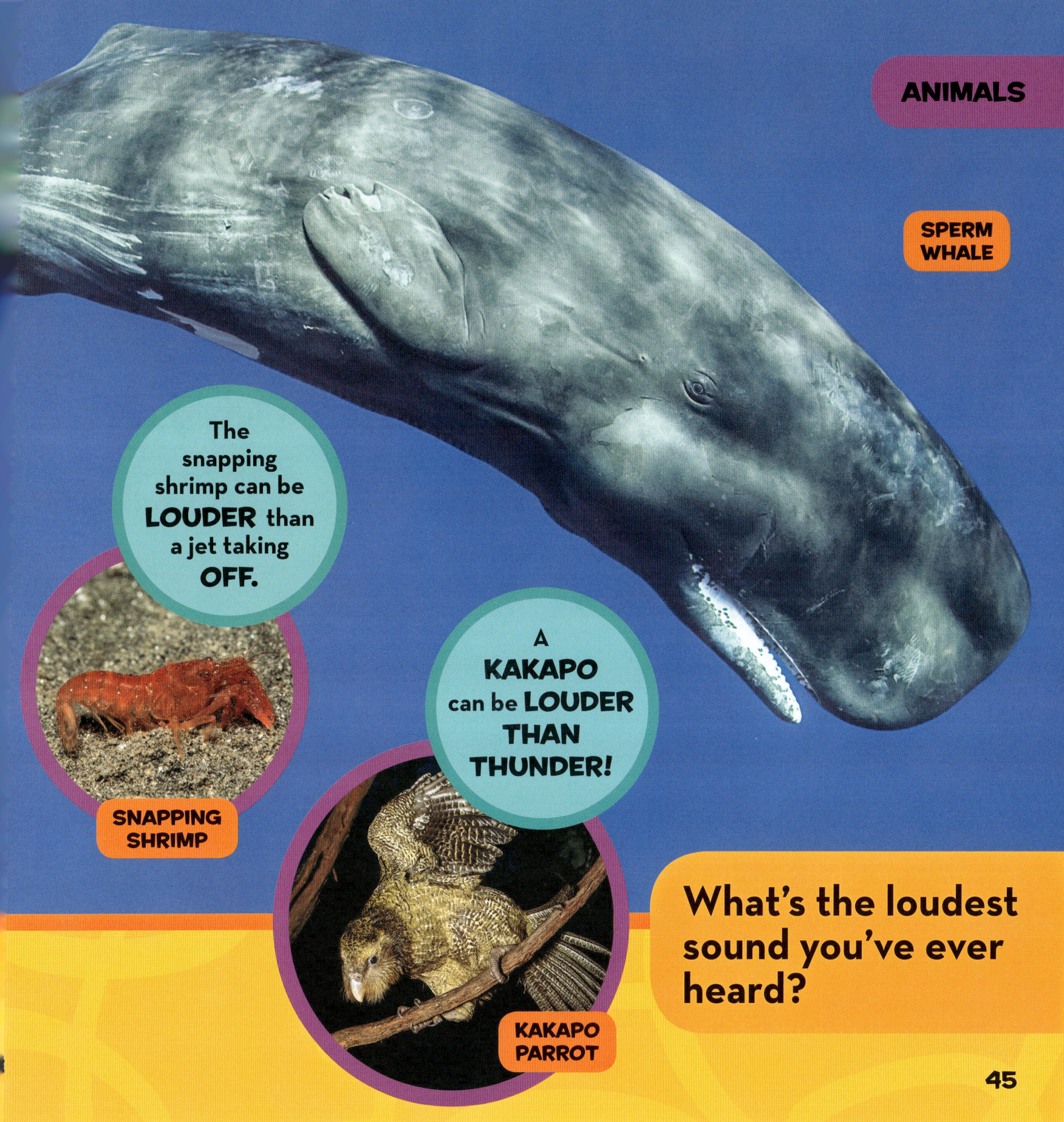

ANIMALS

SPERM WHALE

The snapping shrimp can be **LOUDER** than a jet taking **OFF.**

SNAPPING SHRIMP

A **KAKAPO** can be **LOUDER THAN THUNDER!**

KAKAPO PARROT

What's the loudest sound you've ever heard?

GREEN GROCER CICADA

WHERE DOES THE LOUDEST INSECT LIVE?

Cicadas win the loudest insect award. They are found all over the world. A cicada spends most of its life in the soil, drinking tree sap for food. But when it becomes an adult, it crawls to the surface, into trees and shrubs. Then it sheds its shell-like skin, grows wings, and begins making its loud *buzz-buzz-buzz* sound!

The loudest cicada is the green grocer cicada. It lives near the coast in Australia. Its 120-decibel song can be heard a mile and a half (2.4 km) away.

TRY THIS! MAKE A KAZOO

Cicadas make loud buzzing noises. You can make your own buzzing noises with this homemade kazoo.

YOU'LL NEED

empty toilet-paper tube

markers or stickers

scissors

wax paper

rubber band

1 Decorate the tube with markers or stickers.

2 Have an adult help you cut a circle of wax paper about two inches (5 cm) wider than the end of the tube.

3 Cover one end of the tube with the wax paper. Secure the paper with the rubber band.

4 Sing a loud "do-do-doooo!" into the tube's open end.

Try making different kinds of sounds into your kazoo. What causes the loudest buzzing?

WHERE DO KOALAS LIVE?

To see a koala in the wild, you'll need to take a trip "down under"—to Australia, that is. Koalas live in eastern Australia. These fuzzy animals spend most of their time in eucalyptus trees, climbing, eating leaves, and sleeping.

Koalas are marsupials. A marsupial is an animal that carries its babies in a pouch. Most marsupials live in Australia and nearby islands. The others are found in North and South America.

What are some ways that people carry their babies?

ANIMALS

VIRGINIA OPOSSUM

The Tasmanian devil lives only in Tasmania, a large island south of Australia. This marsupial is calm ... usually.

North America's only marsupial, the Virginia opossum, is about the size of a pet cat.

TASMANIAN DEVIL

MONITO DEL MONTE

Red kangaroos are marsupials that hop through eastern Australia and on nearby islands.

This animal's name, *monito del monte*, means "mountain monkey" in Spanish. But it isn't a monkey. It's a mouse-size marsupial. It lives in forests in parts of Chile and Argentina.

RED KANGAROO

WHERE IS HOME FOR GIANT PANDAS?

Giant pandas live in China. They make their home in cool, wet mountain forests, where they find their favorite food, bamboo. A bamboo shoot is soft on the inside, but it has a tough outer layer. That's no problem for a giant panda. It uses its strong teeth to peel off the tough stuff.

A giant panda spends about 12 hours of every day munching bamboo. Because it eats so much, this creature poops dozens of times a day!

A **NEWBORN** giant **PANDA CUB** is not much longer than your **HAND.**

NEWBORN PANDA

50

ANIMALS

RED PANDA

Red pandas also live in China's mountain forests. About the size of a pet cat, red pandas are much smaller than giant pandas. Red pandas eat bamboo, too, but they also eat fruit, acorns, roots, and eggs.

Can you name some other animals that are black and white?

WHERE DO FISH GO WHEN LAKES AND RIVERS FREEZE?

In some places, winter temperatures get so cold that ice forms on the top of rivers, streams, and lakes. The water right under this layer of ice is too cold for most fish to survive. So they gather near the bottom of the lake or river, where the water is a little warmer, to wait out winter.

Turtles have their own ways of surviving the cold winter months. A turtle that lives mostly on land digs a tunnel-like nest in the ground and snuggles inside to hibernate.

A turtle that lives mostly in water swims down to a river or pond's bottom. It tucks into the mud to hibernate.

Frogs hibernate in winter, too. Those that live in water dig into a muddy bottom like turtles do. A land frog hibernates under a log or dead leaves. Sometimes, parts of its body actually freeze, but that doesn't hurt the frog.

Where is your favorite spot to snuggle when it's cold outside?

ANIMALS

TURTLE SUNNING ITSELF ON A LOG

HIBERNATING FROG

HIBERNATION is like a **LONG NAP**. While an animal hibernates, its **HEARTBEAT** and **BREATHING SLOW DOWN** until spring's warmth "wakes up" its body.

WHERE DO BIRDS SLEEP?

FLAMINGOS often **STAND ON ONE LEG** while they **SLEEP.**

Birds sleep in many different places. They might find a spot high in a tree, low in a shrub, on the ground, or even in shallow water.

PARAKEETS

ANIMALS

PIGEON

Many birds prepare for sleep by fluffing their softest feathers, pulling one leg close to their body, and tucking their beak or bill against themselves. This helps them stay warm.

Birds that like to sleep in trees fluff their feathers, too. And some birds can fly and sleep at the same time!

OWLS hunt at night, so they find a **DARK, LEAFY PLACE** to **SLEEP** during the **DAY.**

How do you get ready to go to sleep?

Some animals **MIGRATE**, or **MOVE**, from one place to another to find **FOOD** or to **MATE**.

WILDEBEESTS

WHERE DO ANIMALS MIGRATE?

Wildebeests live in the Serengeti, a part of Africa that is very dry for a few months every year. When this dry season arrives, herds of wildebeests follow the rains across the land to find green grass to eat.

ANIMALS

Caribou, also called reindeer, spend spring and summer munching away on grasses and plants in North America, Europe, Asia, and Greenland. When fall arrives and plant growth slows or stops, the caribou walk hundreds of miles south to find food. In spring, the herds migrate north, back to where their journey began.

Humpback whales spend the summer swimming in cold waters like the Arctic Ocean, eating tons of tiny, shrimplike creatures called krill. In fall, they migrate toward warm waters to have their babies.

CARIBOU

A **CARIBOU HERD** can have as many as **HALF A MILLION** caribou.

KRILL

HUMPBACK WHALES

Some insects migrate, too. Monarch butterflies are the long-distance champs. Each fall, some monarch butterflies travel almost 3,000 miles (4,800 km) from Canada and the northeastern United States to Southern California or central Mexico, where it is warm. Millions of monarchs spend the winter there, clustered on tree branches.

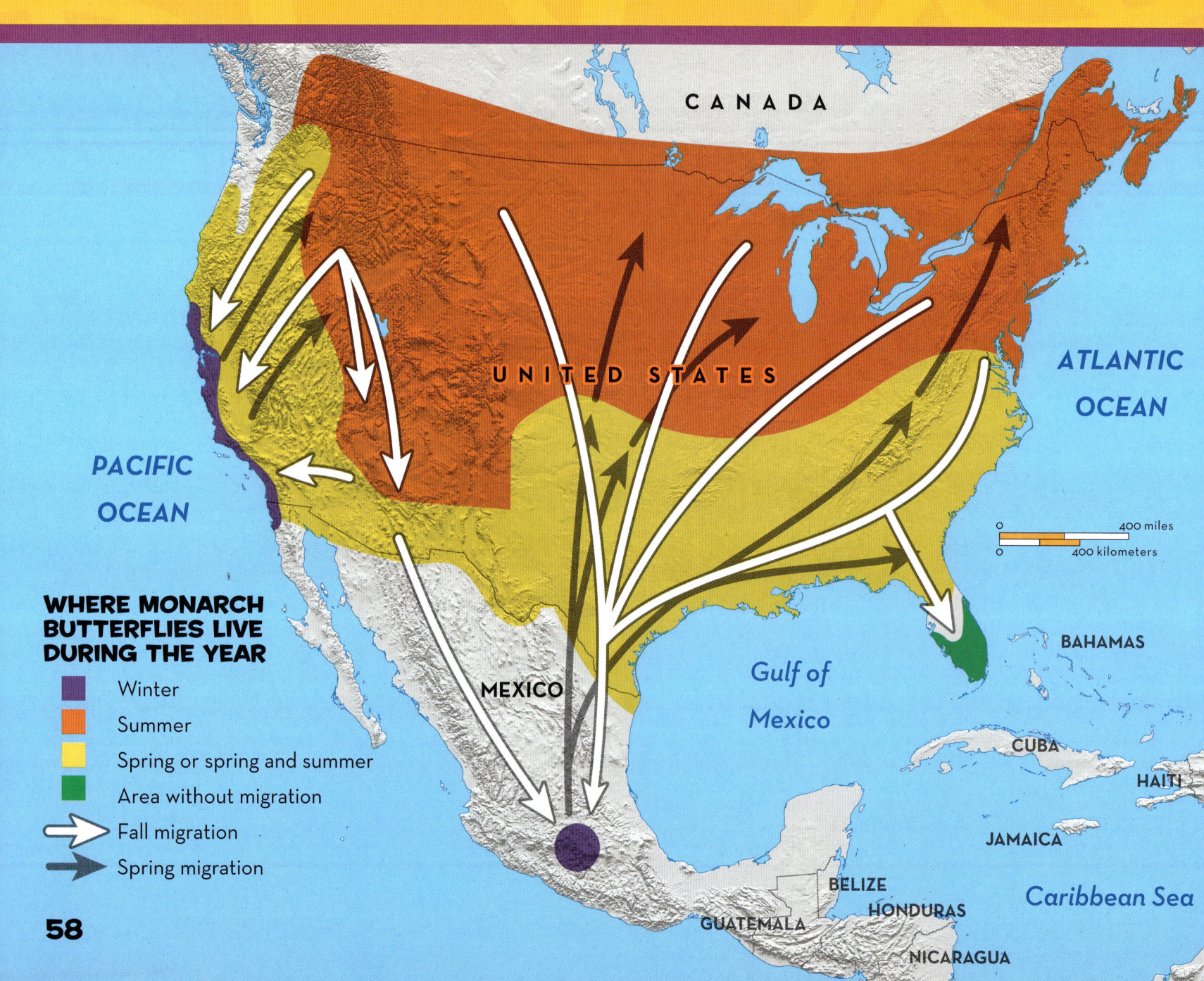

ANIMALS

When spring arrives, the monarchs begin the trip north. They stop along the way, living just long enough to lay their eggs.

Those eggs hatch into caterpillars that eventually become butterflies. These new butterflies then fly another few hundred miles north and stop to lay their own eggs.

Eventually a new generation of monarch butterflies arrives in the north for the warm summer months, until it's time to fly south again.

What is the farthest away from home you've traveled?

MONARCH BUTTERFLY CATERPILLAR

MONARCH BUTTERFLIES

WHERE DID PEOPLE FIRST HAVE PETS?

Nobody knows for sure where people first had pets. Historians *think* it was in parts of Africa and Asia, between 10,000 to 40,000 years ago. They do know that dogs were our first pets. Wild dogs were tamed to stand guard and to help people hunt.

ANCIENT EGYPTIANS were probably the **FIRST** people to have **PET CATS.**

ANIMALS

COUNTRIES WITH THE MOST PET DOGS AND CATS

DOGS
1. United States
2. Brazil
3. China
4. Russia
5. Japan

The friendship between cats and humans also goes back thousands of years, to when people first started storing grain to eat. The grain attracted hungry rats. So when wild cats started hanging around to hunt the rats, humans were happy to have them stay. It helped keep the rats from eating their food.

CATS
1. United States
2. China
3. Russia
4. Brazil
5. France

What is your favorite kind of pet? Why?

POLAR BEAR

WHERE DO ARCTIC ANIMALS GO TO KEEP WARM?

Some Arctic animals, like the arctic fox, the arctic hare, and the polar bear, dig snow dens to escape way-below-zero winter temperatures. As these animals curl up inside their dens, away from icy winds, their thick fur helps hold in body heat. Even the bottoms of their feet are furry!

Arctic swimmers, such as narwhals, seals, and walruses, have a thick, oily layer of fat right under their skin. This fat, called blubber, helps keep body warmth in and cold water temperatures out.

TRY THIS! BLUBBER TEST

YOU'LL NEED
a large bowl
cold water
ice cubes
solid vegetable shortening

Will blubber keep you warm?

1 Fill the bowl about half full of cold water.

2 Add ice cubes until the water is about an inch (2.5 cm) from the top of the bowl.

3 Cover one of your pointer fingers with a thick layer of shortening. Make sure you cover your finger completely. This is your layer of "blubber."

4 Put your two pointer fingers, one bare and one covered with "blubber," into the water. Which finger can you hold in the icy water longer, the one with "blubber," or the one without?

WHERE DO PENGUINS LIVE?

When we see pictures of penguins, they are often standing on ice or snow. That's because many penguins live along Antarctica's frozen coastlines.

But there are 18 different kinds of penguins, and they don't all live in the cold! This map shows where some of these penguins live.

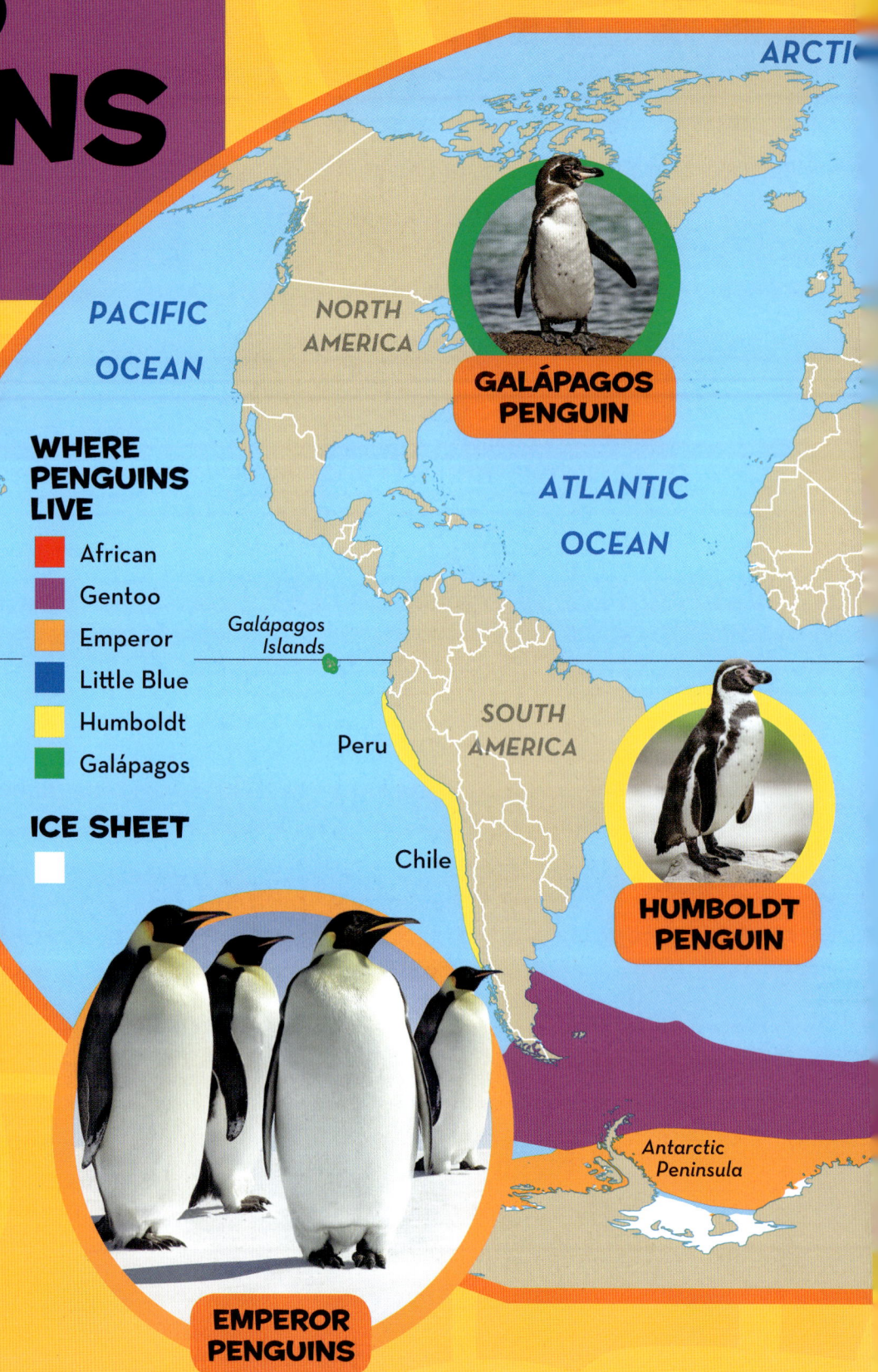

ANIMALS

Which of the **PENGUINS** shown here lives **CLOSEST TO YOU?**

PENGUINS eat food found only in the sea, like **FISH, SQUID,** and **KRILL.** Where does the food you eat come from?

Can you waddle-walk like a penguin?

65

WHERE DO ANIMALS LIVE IN ANTARCTICA?

KING PENGUINS AND SOUTHERN ELEPHANT SEALS

Like penguins, other animals that live in Antarctica stay close to the coastline or live in the ocean. That's where they can find food. They do not live in the continent's chillier interior, where there is no food to eat or water to drink and the land is frozen solid!

Many kinds of seals live along Antarctica's coastline. There are southern fur seals, southern elephant seals, Weddell seals, and leopard seals, just to name a few.

ANIMALS

No **PEOPLE** live in Antarctica year-round. **IT HAS NO TOWNS OR CITIES.** But scientists do visit **RESEARCH STATIONS** where they study the continent's land, weather, and wildlife.

Several kinds of birds fly in Antarctic skies, including blue-eyed shags, snow petrels, snowy sheathbills, and wandering albatross.

The **WANDERING ALBATROSS** has the **WIDEST WINGSPAN** of any bird. Because it is so good at **RIDING THE WIND,** this bird rarely needs to rest—or even **FLAP ITS WINGS!**

WEDDELL SEAL

WANDERING ALBATROSS

67

GOLDEN LION TAMARIN

WHERE ARE WILD MONKEYS FOUND?

Monkeys are divided into two groups, called New World monkeys and Old World monkeys. New World monkeys live in the rainforests of Central and South America. A few of these are the howler monkey, golden lion tamarin, and black spider monkey.

PREHENSILE TAIL

BLACK SPIDER MONKEY

ANIMALS

The **MANDRILL** is the world's **LARGEST MONKEY.** It lives in rainforests in central **AFRICA** and is the size of a **THREE-YEAR-OLD CHILD.**

The world's **SMALLEST MONKEY** is South America's **PYGMY MARMOSET.** It is about the length of your hand.

Most new world monkeys have tails that are *prehensile*. This means that the tail can grab something and hold on.

Old World monkeys, like the baboon, the mandrill, and the Javan langur, are from Africa and Asia. Most Old World monkeys don't have tails.

WHERE DO REAL DRAGONS LIVE?

Dragons live all over the world. Not fire-breathing, storybook dragons, of course, but other animals that are called dragons because of the way they look or behave.

The Komodo dragon is the biggest, heaviest lizard on Earth. It is found only in Indonesia. This giant reptile eats large prey such as water buffalo, deer, and wild boars. A Komodo has a long tongue that constantly flits in and out of its mouth. That's how it tastes the air to "smell" prey.

An **ADULT KOMODO DRAGON** is **LONGER** than your **BED!**

ANIMALS

Called the **SHOCKING PINK DRAGON MILLIPEDE**, this leggy creature lives in Thailand's limestone **CAVES.**

The beautiful **BLUE DRAGON SEA SLUG** rides the ocean waves upside down! This **DRAGON** is no longer than your thumb, but it has a **POISONOUS STING.**

WHERE DID TYRANNOSAURUS REX ROAM?

Tyrannosaurus rex stomped through the ancient forests of western North America. Scientists know this because they have found fossilized bones from *Tyrannosaurus rex*, also called *T. rex*, in these places. This map shows where on Earth some dinosaurs lived millions of years ago.

Which dinosaur is your favorite? Why?

ARCTIC

NORTH AMERICA

Tyrannosaurus rex, Montana, U.S.A.

Triceratops, Colorado, U.S.A.

PACIFIC OCEAN

ATLANTIC OCEAN

SOUTH AMERICA

Giganotosaurus, Argentina

ANIMALS

Archaeopteryx, Germany

OCEAN

EUROPE

ASIA

Velociraptor, Gobi desert, Mongolia

Spinosaurus, Egypt

AFRICA

PACIFIC OCEAN

EQUATOR

INDIAN OCEAN

AUSTRALIA

ANTARCTICA

T. REX FOSSIL

A **FOSSIL** is part of a **LIVING THING** that has been preserved, or saved, in **ROCK.**

This map shows the modern-day names for the areas where **DINOSAURS** once roamed.

73

MAP FUN!

This map shows where some of the awesome animals you met in Chapter Two live in the wild. Use your finger to draw a line from each clue to the animal it describes.

A. The largest land animal
B. The biggest reptile
C. The heaviest snake
D. The loudest insect
E. The heaviest lizard
F. The largest monkey
G. The smallest monkey

WHERE ANIMALS LIVE
- African elephant
- Green anaconda
- Green grocer cicada
- Komodo dragon
- Mandrill
- Pygmy marmoset
- Saltwater crocodile

Which **CONTINENT** has the most **MARSUPIALS**? (Hint: Look on page 48.)

74

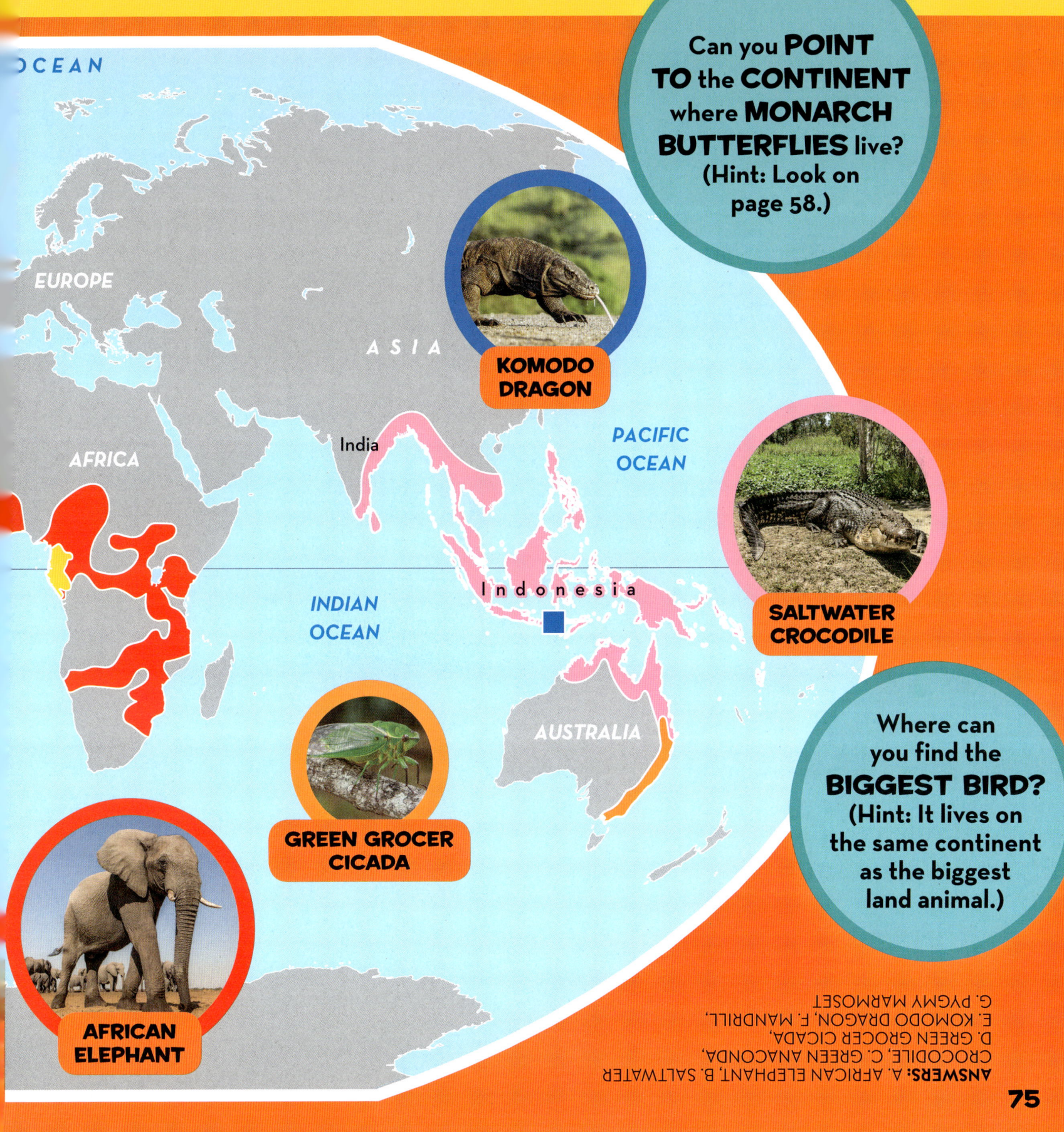

CHAPTER 3
WHERE DID THAT COME FROM?

Surfers catch ocean waves all over the world.

From surfboards to books to pizza, inventions have made our lives easier, more interesting, and even more delicious. This chapter explores where some of these discoveries came from.

WHERE WAS PIZZA INVENTED?

People around the world have been eating flat, warm bread topped with bits of meat and vegetables for hundreds of years. But the pizza we know today—with tomato sauce and gooey cheeses—was invented in Italy.

What do you like to eat on your pizza?

INVENTIONS

Pizza dough is **PUSHED** and **FOLDED,** or kneaded, for a few minutes to make it both **STRONG** and **SOFT.**

TOSSING DOUGH into the **AIR** helps **STRETCH** it out so that it's big enough for the pan.

Legend has it that in 1889, the owner of a restaurant in Naples, Italy, created a new kind of pizza. He wanted to impress the visiting king and queen. This pizza-maker topped his pizza with tomato sauce, mozzarella cheese, and basil. Queen Margherita loved it! A pizza with these three ingredients is still called a "Margherita" today.

MAKE MINE SQUID!

Everybody has their own idea of what makes a pizza yummy. Here are some popular toppings from around the world.

Japan	squid, eel
Costa Rica	coconut
Brazil	peas
Pakistan	curry
India	pickled ginger
Sweden	peanuts
Australia	shrimp
U.S.A.	pepperoni
Iceland	bananas

KULFI

MOCHI

Different countries have their own delicious **ICE-CREAM-LIKE** treats. In Italy, it's **GELATO**. India has **KULFI**. And in Japan, you can enjoy **MOCHI**.

Another tasty treat, ice cream, is one of the best food inventions ever! But where was it first made?

INVENTIONS

Ice cream was invented in China nearly 1,400 years ago. That ice cream was probably made using buffalo milk and didn't look or taste much like the stuff we eat today. It was more like a slushy drink or a snow cone.

YUM! This chart shows where some popular foods were invented.

hot dogs	Germany
french fries	Belgium
tacos	Mexico
chocolate candy bars	England
dumplings	China
granola bars	United States

What is your favorite food?

WHERE WERE THE FIRST BOOKS MADE?

Ancient Egyptians were the first to write words on paper-like material for people to read. Called papyrus, this thick material was made from the papyrus plant.

PAPYRUS

About 2,000 years ago, the Chinese invented a light, thin paper. They bound paper pages together into books. But those early Chinese books were all written by hand.

The first books that look like the ones we know today were made in Korea, on a machine called a printing press. It worked by pressing sheets of paper against tiny blocks with raised characters. These blocks, called movable type, had ink on them. Now books no longer had to be copied by hand!

Can you figure out where this book was printed? (HINT: Look on the last page.)

INVENTIONS

PRINTING PRESS

Today, books are **PRINTED ALL OVER THE WORLD** using computer **TECHNOLOGY.**

83

OUTDOOR SET

WHERE ARE TV SHOWS MADE?

Television shows are made all over the world. People called actors put on a show while cameras record them. The area where actors film the show is called a set.

Sometimes sets are inside very large buildings. That's partly because it takes a lot of people to make a TV show: makeup artists, set and costume designers, set builders, and those who work on the lights, microphones, and cameras. These people are called the crew. We don't see them when we watch a show, but it couldn't go on without them!

On the set, carpenters build rooms that look like the inside of a real house or office. They don't build the entire house. On set, rooms are missing walls and ceilings! Also, many doors lead to … nothing.

INVENTIONS

INDOOR SET

On some shows, you can **HEAR** people **LAUGHING** or noises like birds **CHIRPING**. These **SOUNDS** are usually **ADDED** after the show is filmed and before you see it on **TV**.

CARTOONS are **ANIMATED SHOWS**. They are made up of **THOUSANDS** of still pictures. When the **PICTURES** are **SHOWN QUICKLY** in a certain order, it looks like the objects in them are **MOVING!**

WHERE WERE BICYCLES INVENTED?

The first bicycle was invented in Germany about 200 years ago. It had no pedals. To make it go, riders had to place their feet on the ground and push, push, push!

Early bicycles were made from wood or steel. They were heavy and hard to hold up. Their wheels were covered with leather or iron. Because riders felt every bump, these bicycles were nicknamed "boneshakers." Rubber tires came along in the 1880s to help smooth the ride. Whew!

Bikes got pedals in the 1860s. They were connected to the front wheel. A few years later, an English inventor figured out how to use a chain to connect those pedals to the rear wheel. Bikes finally got brakes, too.

PUSH BICYCLE

A "HIGH WHEEL" bicycle was invented in FRANCE in the 1860s. You needed LONG LEGS to RIDE it!

INVENTIONS

SKATEBOARDS were invented by **SURFERS** looking for a way to practice on **LAND.** Someone in California, U.S.A., attached **OLD ROLLER SKATES** to a short wooden board, and **SIDEWALK SURFING** began. Cool, dude!

SKATEBOARD

Like the bicycle, the kick scooter was also invented in Germany. The first kick scooters had small wheels and were made from scraps of wood.

SCOOTER

How many other things with wheels can you name?

INVENTIONS

SURFBOARD

Some **DOGS** and **CATS** surf, too. Dogs even have their own **WORLD SURFING** championships!

Surfboards were invented about 1,500 years ago by the people of Polynesia—an area in the Pacific Ocean made up of hundreds of islands. The first surfboards were wooden and weighed more than 100 pounds (45 kg).

WHERE WERE BOARD GAMES INVENTED?

People have been playing games by moving pieces on boards for a long, long time. Here are where some popular games came from.

Checkers was first played in the land now known as Iraq. Depending on where the game is played, the game board can have 64, 100, or 144 squares.

Mancala has been around for so long that nobody knows exactly where it started.

Go is a game that is popular throughout Asia. It was invented in China about 4,000 years ago.

INVENTIONS

Candy Land was introduced in 1949 by a woman in California, who had invented the game while she was sick in a hospital.

Backgammon started in the land now known as Iraq.

Chess began in India and soon spread around the world.

Ancient Egyptians played a board game called senet.

What board games do you like to play?

WHERE DOES THE WATER GO WHEN I FLUSH?

SEWAGE TREATMENT PLANT

When you flush a toilet, a force called gravity pulls the water down. *Whoosh! Glug-glug-glug.* The water travels through underground pipes until it reaches a place called a sewage treatment plant.

In the treatment plant, the water flows through a screen to remove trash. The water is cleaned over and over again before it is released into local rivers or streams.

INVENTIONS

England was the first country to have toilets inside the house. Before that, people used little buildings in their backyards called outhouses. Their pee and poop would fall down into a pit. When the pit got full, the family would move the outhouse to a freshly dug pit and fill the old one with dirt.

OUTHOUSE

Before **TOILET PAPER** was invented, people around the world used bits of **NEWSPAPER,** shells, **LEAVES,** corncobs, sheep's wool, or whatever was **HANDY.**

WHERE DOES OUR GARBAGE GO?

Have you ever wondered where a garbage truck takes your trash? It depends on where you live. In some places, trash is hauled to special plants where it is burned to make power. In other places, it goes into a machine that breaks it down into tiny pieces. Some goes to recycling centers to be sorted.

But most household trash goes to a landfill. At a landfill, huge bulldozers and loaders push dirt over trash piles all day long. Mountains of buried trash get higher and higher.

Modern **GARBAGE TRUCKS** were invented in the **U.S.** in the early **1900S.**

RECYCLED PLASTIC BOTTLES can be made into shopping **BAGS,** T-shirts and sweaters, insulation for **COATS** and sleeping bags, and **CARPETING.**

INVENTIONS

Inside the landfill, some things—food, paper, rope, clothing—will break down, or decompose, in a few months or years. Other things—plastic, tin cans, shoes, diapers—take many, many years to decompose. Recycling is an important way to help reduce trash in landfills.

QUEENSLAND, AUSTRALIA

LANDFILL

When you make something **NEW** and **USEFUL** out of something old, it's called **UPCYCLING**. Upcycling is another way to help our planet stay cleaner. **TRASH** can even be made **INTO ART!**

MAP FUN!

This map shows where some favorite foods first came from. With your finger, draw a line from the picture of each food to the place where that food was invented.

A. Pizza
B. Ice cream
C. Hot dogs
D. French fries
E. Tacos
F. Chocolate candy bars
G. Dumplings

Where did people first play **CHESS?** (Hint: Look at page 91.)

CHAPTER 4
WHERE CAN I FIND THAT?

People enjoy a roller coaster at Liseberg amusement park in Gothenberg, Sweden.

From amazing sports stadiums to supersized art, from upside-down houses to rocking roller coasters, find out where some of the world's most unusual places and things can be found.

RUNGRADO MAY DAY STADIUM

WHERE IS THE BIGGEST SPORTS STADIUM?

The world's biggest outdoor stadium is the Rungrado May Day Stadium in Pyongyang, North Korea. It has seating for more than 100,000 people. Soccer games and other sporting events are held here. But the stadium is most famous for hosting a dance performance that includes more than 100,000 dancers.

UNUSUAL PLACES

People who like eating hot dogs at games might want to see the **GIANT HOT DOG** in Michigan, U.S.A. It's as long as **120** regular hot dogs. But you can't eat this one. **IT'S ART!**

The Indianapolis Motor Speedway in Indiana, U.S.A., is huge too. This outdoor structure holds a 2.5-mile (4-km)-long racetrack. At the Indianapolis 500, drivers race their cars around the track 200 times. That is a total of 500 miles (805 km)!

INDIANAPOLIS MOTOR SPEEDWAY

WHERE IS THE WORLD'S TALLEST BUILDING?

Tall buildings that reach high into the sky are called skyscrapers. The tallest is the Burj Khalifa, in the United Arab Emirates. It is twice as tall as the Empire State Building in New York City.

The Empire State Building is New York City's most famous landmark. When it opened in 1931, it was the tallest building in the world.

EMPIRE STATE BUILDING

What is the tallest building you have ever seen?

The **BURJ KHALIFA** has one of the **FASTEST ELEVATORS** in the world. It takes only **ONE MINUTE** to travel from the ground floor to the observation deck on the **124TH FLOOR.**

BURJ KHALIFA

UNUSUAL PLACES

The first skyscraper, the Home Insurance Building, was built in 1885 in Chicago, Illinois, U.S.A. It was 10 stories high. A 10-story building might not seem tall now. But at the time, people were amazed that it didn't fall down.

THE HOME INSURANCE BUILDING

Some buildings are famous for being tall. Others are popular because of their beautiful shapes, or because important government work or religious events happen inside them. On these pages are buildings that draw millions of visitors each year.

TAJ MAHAL, AGRA, INDIA

TOWER OF PISA, PISA, ITALY

The **LEANING TOWER OF PISA** was built to be the **BELL TOWER** for a cathedral. It was supposed to **STAND STRAIGHT.** But because it was on sandy ground, the tower quickly started to **LEAN.** What started as an **"UH-OH"** made the tower one of the most famous buildings in the world!

UNUSUAL PLACES

SENSOJI TEMPLE, TOKYO, JAPAN

SAINT BASIL'S CATHEDRAL, MOSCOW, RUSSIA

Because **ROOFS** like those of Saint Basil's Cathedral are shaped like **ONIONS**, they are called **ONION DOMES**.

EIFFEL TOWER, PARIS, FRANCE

WHERE ARE THE MOST MYSTERIOUS PLACES?

Ancient, mysterious places are all around the world. They make us wonder who made them, and how and why they were built.

At Stonehenge, England, people living 4,000 to 5,000 years ago built circles of gigantic standing stones. Over time, many of the stones have fallen down. We don't know how the stones were moved to the area or raised into place—or why the circles were built.

STONEHENGE

UNUSUAL PLACES

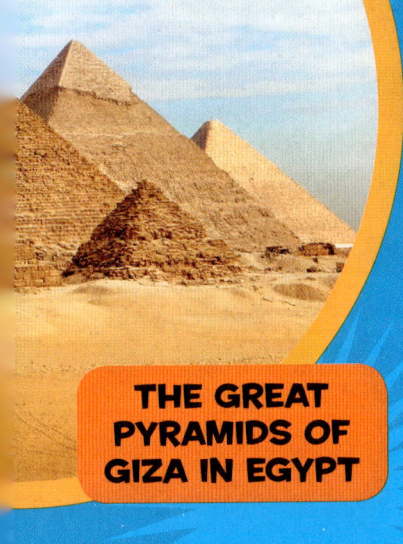

THE GREAT PYRAMIDS OF GIZA IN EGYPT

Many Egyptian pyramids are also more than 4,000 years old. They were often built as burial places for Egyptian royalty. We are still trying to learn how ancient people made these buildings with such heavy stones.

Airplane passengers flying over southern Peru in South America might not believe what they see far below. On the ground are giant drawings of animals, plants, arrows, zigzags, straight lines, and more. These pictures and lines are called the Nasca Lines. They are 2,000 years old. Scientists still don't know why the lines were created or what they mean.

The Nasca Lines include pictures of a **DOG**, a **DUCK**, a **HUMMINGBIRD**, (above), a lizard, a monkey, and even a **WHALE!**

WHERE ARE THE WORLD'S TWISTIEST ROADS?

Imagine a road going straight up a steep mountain. Driving to the top would be impossible for most car engines. Driving down would be even worse, because the brakes would quickly wear out. So instead, mountain roads are built in a back-and-forth, twisty way that is much easier on cars. Here are some of the world's twistiest roads.

This **HIGHWAY** is called the Transfagarasan mountain road. It loops and **WRIGGLES** through **MOUNTAINS** in **ROMANIA**.

UNUSUAL PLACES

A super-SHARP TURN in a ROAD is called a SWITCHBACK.

Grimsel Pass is a winding road that hugs the side of a mountain in Switzerland.

The Big Gate Road in China took eight years to build. This road has 99 sharp turns!

DUGE BEIPANJIANG BRIDGE

WHERE IS THE WORLD'S HIGHEST BRIDGE?

The Duge Beipanjiang Bridge in southwest China is the highest in the world. It rises 1,854 feet (565 m) above the Beipan River. That's so high you could almost stack two of France's Eiffel Towers underneath it!

What is the highest bridge you've crossed?

UNUSUAL PLACES

MOSES BRIDGE

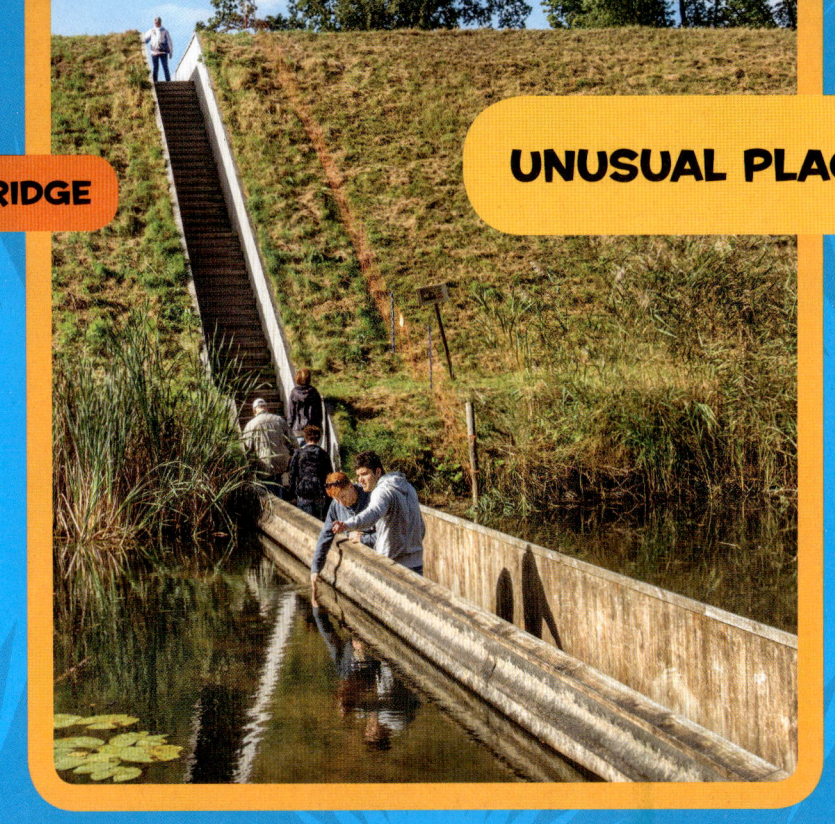

The Moses Bridge in the Netherlands doesn't go over the water—it goes right through it!

London, England, is home to the Rolling Bridge. Once a week, operators unroll the bridge so people can walk over the Grand Union Canal.

Pakistan's Hussaini Hanging Bridge, made of ropes and wooden boards, should be crossed one careful step at a time!

ROLLING BRIDGE

HUSSAINI HANGING BRIDGE

WHERE IS THE TALLEST FERRIS WHEEL?

The world's tallest Ferris wheel is the High Roller in Las Vegas, Nevada, U.S.A. At the top, riders are 550 feet (168 m) in the air. That's about as high as a 50-story building!

People rode the first Ferris wheel at the world's fair in Chicago, Illinois, in 1893. It was named for its inventor, George Ferris, Jr. His wheel was 25 stories high and held more than 2,000 passengers.

HIGH ROLLER FERRIS WHEEL

UNUSUAL PLACES

FORMULA ROSSA

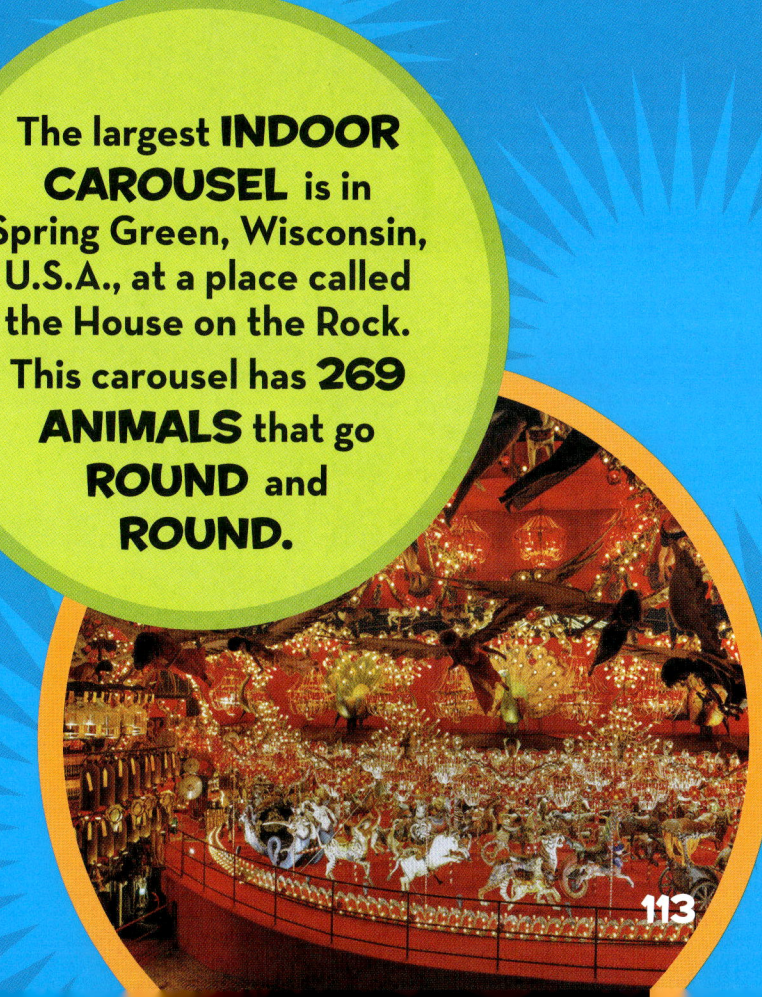

The fastest roller coaster is the Formula Rossa, in Abu Dhabi, United Arab Emirates. It speeds around the track so fast that riders have to wear goggles to protect their eyes!

At the time this book was written, the tallest roller coaster was the Kingda Ka, in New Jersey. It's taller than a 40-story building!

KINGDA KA

The largest **INDOOR CAROUSEL** is in Spring Green, Wisconsin, U.S.A., at a place called the House on the Rock. This carousel has **269 ANIMALS** that go **ROUND** and **ROUND**.

THE TROPICAL ISLANDS

WHERE ARE THE COOLEST THEME PARKS?

Many theme parks offer unusual rides and attractions. Here are a few that have some extra surprises in store.

UNUSUAL PLACES

The Tropical Islands theme park near Berlin, Germany, is the world's largest indoor water park. Visitors can pitch a tent and camp in a human-made rainforest, float in a hot-air balloon, or swim and splash on sandy beaches—even in the winter!

At Diggerland theme parks in the United Kingdom and the United States, kids can dig for hidden treasure behind the wheel of a mini-excavator, steer a steamroller, or learn to drive a real digger.

Bollywood Parks, in Dubai, United Arab Emirates, has thrilling rides and a stage show with rhythmic music, sparkling lights, and dancers in colorful, swirling costumes.

DIGGERLAND

BOLLYWOOD PARKS

TOKYO DISNEYLAND

Part of DisneySea is made to look like Venice, Italy, with **WATER CANALS** and **GONDOLAS.**

U.S.A.'s Disneyland and Walt Disney World are the most popular theme parks in the world. But number three on the list is Japan's Tokyo Disneyland! This park includes DisneySea, where visitors can enjoy all sorts of water rides and adventures. Kids can even explore the Little Mermaid's playground.

UNUSUAL PLACES

At Efteling, a theme park in the Netherlands, visitors can explore enchanted forests complete with colorful elves and fairies. Other parts of the park bring storybooks to life, including Hansel and Gretel, Snow White, and more.

A tree in Efteling **SPEAKS TO VISITORS.**

EFTELING PARK

If you could design a theme park, what would it be like?

WHERE IS THE MOST FUN PLACE TO LIVE?

Any place can be fun if you make it that way. The upside-down house in Trassenheide, Germany, makes a lot of people smile. Everything inside the house is upside-down, too. People couldn't really live here, but they like to stop in and take a stroll on the ceiling!

TRY THIS! BUILD A HOUSE OF CARDS

YOU'LL NEED

a deck of playing cards

a tabletop

Building any kind of house takes careful planning. Every piece must fit together perfectly. For fun, try building a house made of cards. How high will your house get before it collapses?

1 The base: Lean two cards against each other in the shape of an upside-down V.

2 Make two more Vs beside the first, so you have a row of three upside-down Vs.

3 Lay cards flat atop the Vs, as pictured.

4 Build more Vs atop the flat cards, as pictured.

5 Repeat the steps, until … oops! The cards all fall.

MAP FUN!

This map shows where to find some of the amazing places you read about in Chapter Four. With your finger, draw a line from each clue to the place it describes.

A. The biggest sports stadium

B. The tallest building

C. A tower that looks like it's falling over

D. A cathedral with onion-shaped domes

E. Two circles of gigantic standing stones

F. Giant drawings on the ground

G. The highest bridge

H. The highest Ferris wheel

A.

C.

High Roller, Nevada, U.S.A

NORTH AMERICA

ATLANTIC OCEAN

PACIFIC OCEAN

G.

Nasca Lines, Peru

SOUTH AMERICA

ATLANTIC OCEAN

E.

Which of these **PLACES** would you like to **VISIT FIRST? WHY?**

PARENT TIPS

Extend your child's experience beyond the pages of this book. Visit art galleries, museums, zoos, and even theme parks. Exploring the world with your child provides endless opportunities to teach and to learn. Here are some other activities you can do with National Geographic's *Little Kids First Big Book of Where*.

TRAVEL PLANS!
(GEOGRAPHY)
Take a look at a globe or a world map and help your child find where she lives. Then help her plan a route to one or more of the places in the book. Trace routes traveling on water and traveling on land.

TASTE TEST
(INVESTIGATION)
Komodo dragons "taste" by flicking their tongues. Place a blindfold over your child's eyes and have him flick his tongue at a variety of dry foods you've assembled on a clean surface— cereal, mini marshmallows, bits of granola bar, shredded cheese, and others. How many can he identify without looking?

KNOCK-KNOCK!
(COMMUNICATION)
Some whales communicate with each other by using a pattern of clicks. Brainstorm and write down four to five knocking patterns with your child and decide what each one means—things like *I'm hungry* or *I'm thirsty* or *Come over here*. Then take turns knocking patterns on a hard surface to see

if you can understand each other.

THE FUN HOUSE
(ARTS AND CRAFTS)
Some people around the world live in unique-looking homes. Have your child imagine a funny house she'd like to live in, then draw and color it. Ask her to write a silly story set in that house.

WHAT'S YOUR WINGSPAN?
(MATH)
The albatross has the widest wingspan of any bird on Earth—about 11 feet (3 m). Have your child stand with his arms straight out to his sides. With a tape measure or yard stick, measure his "wingspan" from one hand's fingertips to the other's. Then let him guess whether *your* wingspan will be greater or less than his own. Compare your wingspans to that of an albatross.

FALLING WATERS
(OBSERVATION)
Waterfalls look different depending on the amount of water and where it's falling from. Help your child play with this concept by pouring water from various sizes and shapes of plastic containers into a sink or a bathtub.

GLOSSARY

CONIFEROUS trees and shrubs that have cones and needle-shaped leaves

DECIDUOUS plants or trees that lose their leaves for part of the year

ERUPT to suddenly gush, like lava or ash does from a volcano

GLACIER a slow-moving mass of ice usually found high up in mountains or near the poles

GRAVITY the force that pulls things toward Earth

LANDMASS a large chunk of land, such as a continent or a large island

POLYP a tiny sea creature with a cylinder-shaped body and a mouth surrounded by small tentacles

RAINFOREST a forest where rain falls often, making it rich with plant and animal life

SANDSTONE a kind of rock made up of tiny grains of sand or quartz

SEWAGE human waste

WINGSPAN the tip-to-tip measurement of a bird's outspread wings

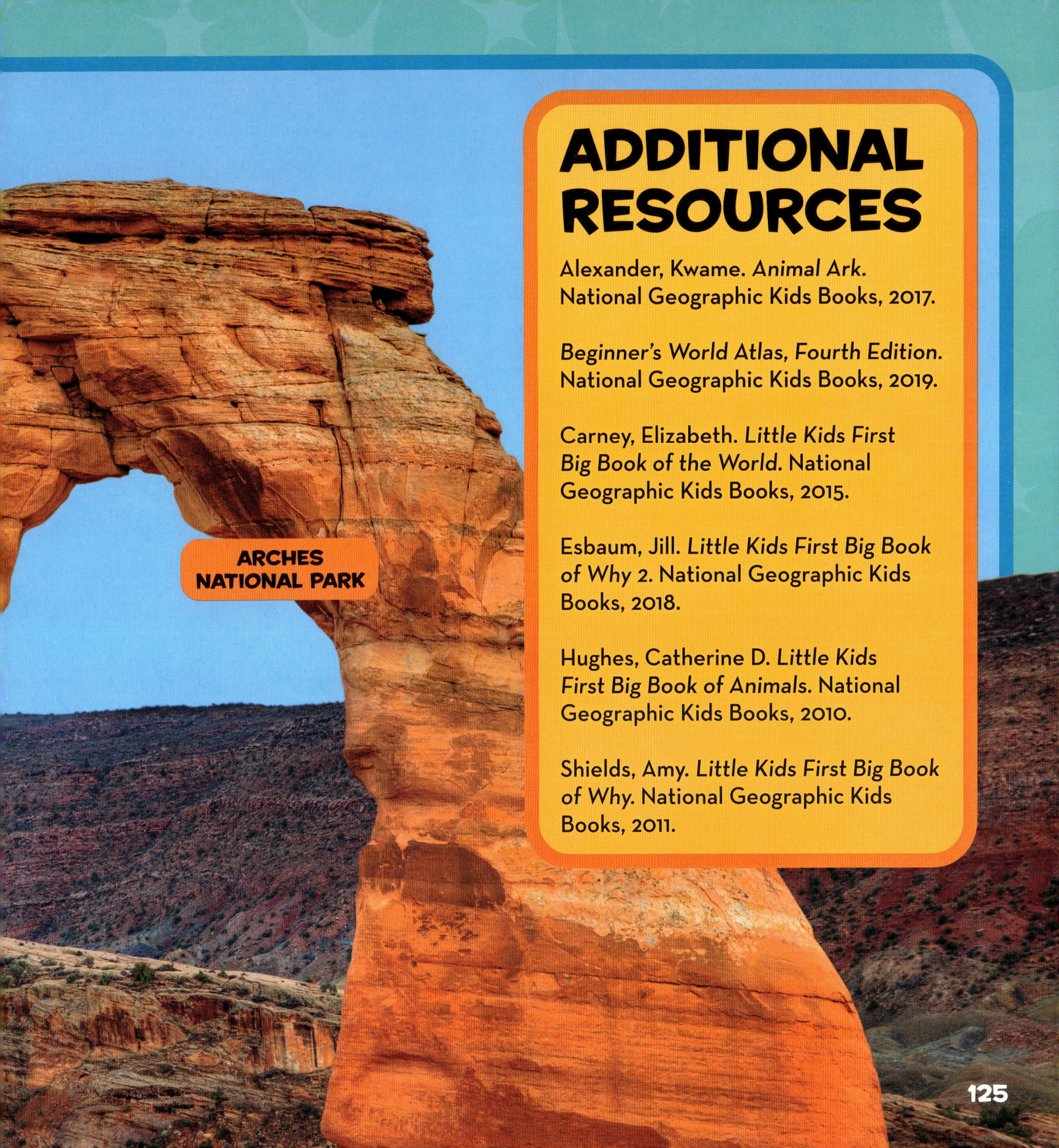

ARCHES NATIONAL PARK

ADDITIONAL RESOURCES

Alexander, Kwame. *Animal Ark*. National Geographic Kids Books, 2017.

Beginner's World Atlas, Fourth Edition. National Geographic Kids Books, 2019.

Carney, Elizabeth. *Little Kids First Big Book of the World*. National Geographic Kids Books, 2015.

Esbaum, Jill. *Little Kids First Big Book of Why 2*. National Geographic Kids Books, 2018.

Hughes, Catherine D. *Little Kids First Big Book of Animals*. National Geographic Kids Books, 2010.

Shields, Amy. *Little Kids First Big Book of Why*. National Geographic Kids Books, 2011.

INDEX

Boldface indicates illustrations.

A
African elephants 40, **40**, 74, **75**
African lions 44, **44**
African penguins 64, **65**
Albatrosses 67, **67**, **122**, 123
Amazon rainforest, South America 22-23, **22-23**, 36
Amazon River, South America 31, **31**
Amusement parks **98-99**, 114-117, **114-117**
Angel Falls, Venezuela 32, **32**
Antarctica **28**, 66, 67
   animals 66-67, **66-67**
   glaciers 26, **26**, 37
   research stations 67, **67**
   as world's biggest desert 28
Archaeopteryx **73**
Arches National Park, Utah, U.S.A. 25, **25**, **124-125**
Arctic animals 62
Atacama Desert, Chile **4-5**, 29, **29**, 36
Aurora australis 35, **35**
Aurora borealis **2-3**, 35, **35**
Ayers Rock, Australia 24-25, **24-25**, 37

B
Backgammon 91, **91**
Bamboo 50, 51
Bicycles 86, **86**, **87**, 88, 97
Big Gate Road, China 109, **109**
Birds: sleep **54**, 54-55, **55**
Black spider monkeys 69, **69**
Blood Falls (glacier), Antarctica 26, **26**
Blubber 62, 63
Blue dragon sea slugs 71, **71**
Blue morpho butterflies 23
Blue whales 40, **40**
Board games 90-91, **90-91**
Bollywood Parks, Dubai, United Arab Emirates 115, **115**
Books 82, 83, **83**

Burj Khalifa, Dubai, United Arab Emirates **1-2**, 102, **102-103**, 103, **121**

C
Camels 29, **29**
Candy Land (game) 91, **91**
Cards, house of 119, **119**
Caribou **38-39**, 57, **57**
Carousels 113, **113**
Cartoons 85
Caterpillars 59, **59**
Cats 61, **61**, 89
Caves 10, 20-21, **20-21**, 71
Challenger Deep, Mariana Trench, Pacific Ocean 16
Checkers 90, **90**
Chess 91, **91**, 96
Chocolate candy bars 81, **81**, 96
Cicadas 46, **46**, 47, 74, **75**
Coral reefs 13, **13**

D
Deserts **28**, 28-29, **29**, 36
Diggerland theme parks 115, **115**
Dinosaurs 72, **72**, 73
Dogs 60, **60**, 61, **61**, 89, **89**
Dragons 70-71, **70-71**
Duge Beipanjiang Bridge, China 110, **110**, 120
Dumplings 81, **81**, 97

E
Earthquakes 18
Efteling (theme park), Netherlands 117, **117**
Egyptians, ancient
   board game 91, **91**
   papyrus 82, **82**
   pet cats 61
   pyramids 107
Eiffel Tower, Paris, France **105**
Emperor penguins 64, **64**
Empire State Building, New York City, New York 102, **102**
Everest, Mount, China-Nepal 14-15, **14-15**, 36, 37

F
Fennec foxes 29, **29**
Ferris wheels 112, **112**, 120
Fish 16, **16**, 52, **52**
Flamingos 54, **54**
Formula Rossa, Abu Dhabi, United Arab Emirates 113, **113**
Fossils 72, 73, **73**
French fries 81, **81**, 96
Frogs 53, **53**

G
Galápagos penguins 64, **64**
Garbage 94-95, **94-95**
Gelato 80
Gentoo penguins 64, **65**
Giant pandas 50, **50-51**
Giant river otters 23
Giganotosaurus 72
Giraffes 41, **41**
Giza, Egypt: pyramids **106-107**
Glaciers 26, **26**, 36, **37**, 124
Go (game) 90, **90-91**
Golden lion tamarins 68, **68**
Granola bars 81, **81**
Green anacondas 42, **42**, 74, **74**
Green grocer cicadas 46, **46**, 74, **75**
Grimsel Pass, Switzerland 109, **109**

H
Hang Son Doong (cave), Vietnam 10, 20, **20-21**
Hibernation 53
High Roller (Ferris wheel), Las Vegas, Nevada, U.S.A. 112, **112**, **121**
Hoatzins 22
Home Insurance Building, Chicago, Illinois, U.S.A. 103, **103**
Hot dogs
   food 81, **81**, 97, **97**
   supersized art 101, **101**
Humboldt penguins 64, **64**
Humpback whales 57, **57**
Hussaini Hanging Bridge, Pakistan 111, **111**

I
Ice cream 80, **80**, 81, 96
Ice cubes
   blubber test 63, **63**
   melting 27, **27**
Indianapolis Motor Speedway, Indiana, U.S.A. 101, **101**
Insects 23, 41, **41**, 46, **46**, 58

J
Jellyfish 16, **16**

K
Kakapo parrots 44, **45**
Kazoos 47, **47**
Khone Falls, Laos 33, **33**, 37
King cobras 43, **43**
King penguins **66-67**
Kingda Ka (roller coaster), New Jersey, U.S.A. 113, **113**
Koalas 48, **48**
Komodo dragons 70, **70-71**, 74, **75**, **122**, **123**
Krill 57, **57**, 65
Kulfi 80, **80**

L
Lambert-Fisher Glacier, Antarctica 26, **26**, 37
Landfills 94-95, **94-95**
Liseberg amusement park, Gothenberg, Sweden **98-99**
Little blue penguins 64, **65**

M
Mammoth Cave, Kentucky, U.S.A. 20, **20**
Mancala 90, **90**
Mandrills 69, **69**, 74, **74**
Maps, world
   animals 74-75
   dinosaurs 72-73
   inventions 96-97
   Mid-Ocean Ridge 15
   natural wonders 36-37
   oceans 12
   penguins 64-65
   physical map 9
   political map 8
   Ring of Fire 18
   unusual places 120-121
Margherita, Queen (Italy) 79
Mariana Trench, Pacific Ocean 16
Marsupials **48**, 48-49, **49**, 74
Mid-Ocean Ridge 15
Milky Way 34, **34**
Mochi 80, **80**
Monarch butterflies 58-59, **59**, 75
   caterpillars 59, **59**
   migration map 58
Monitos del monte 49, **49**
Monkeys 68-69, **68-69**, 74, **74**
Moses Bridge, Netherlands 111, **111**

N
Nasca Lines, Peru 107, **107**, 121, **121**
Night sky 34, **34**
Nile River, Africa **30**, 31
Northern lights **2-3**, 35, **35**

O
Oceans 12-13
Ostriches 41, **41**
Outhouses 93, **93**
Owls 55, **55**

P
Papyrus 82, **82**, 97
Parakeets 55, **55**
Penguins **64**, 64-65, **65**, 66
Pets **60**, 60-61, **61**
Pigeons 55, **55**
Pizza **78**, 78-79, **96**
Polar bears 62, **62**
Polyps 13, **13**, 124
Printing presses 82, **82-83**
Pygmy marmosets 69, **69**, 74, **74**
Pyramids **106-107**, 107
Pythons 42, **42**

R
Rainforests 22-23, **22-23**, **36**, 124
Recycling 94, 95
Red kangaroos 49, **49**
Red pandas 51, **51**
Ring of Fire 18
Roller coasters **98-99**, 113, **113**
Rolling Bridge, London, England 111, **111**
Rungrado May Day Stadium, Pyongyang, North Korea 100, **100-101**, 120

S
Sac Actun (cave), Mexico 21, **21**
Sahara, Africa 29, **29**, 36
Saint Basil's Cathedral, Moscow, Russia 105, **105**, 121
Saltwater crocodiles 41, **41**, 74, **75**
Sandstone 25, 124
Scooters 88, **88**
Senet (board game) 91, **91**
Sensoji Temple, Tokyo, Japan 105
Sewage treatment plants 92, **92-93**
Shocking pink dragon millipedes **70-71**, 71
Skateboards 88, **88**, 97
Skyscrapers **1-2**, 102-103, **102-103**
Sleep: birds 54, 54-55, **55**
Snailfish 16, **16**
Snakes 42, **42**, 42-43, **43**, 74, **74**
Snapping shrimp 44, **45**
Southern elephant seals 66, **66-67**
Southern lights 35, **35**
Sperm whales 44, **44-45**
Spinosaurus 73
Spiny devil katydids 23
Stick insects 41, **41**
Stonehenge, England 106, **106-107**, 120, **120**
Submersibles 16, **17**
Surfboards **77**, 89, **89**

T
Tacos 81, **81**, 97
Taj Mahal, Agra, India **104-105**
Tasmanian devils 49, **49**
Television shows
 crews **84**, 85
 sets **84**, 84-85, **85**
 sounds 85
Theme parks 114-117, **114-117**
Titan beetles 23
Toilets 92, 93
Tokyo Disneyland, Japan 116, **116**
Tower of Pisa, Italy 104, **104**, 120

Transfagarasan mountain road, Romania 108, **108-109**
Triceratops 72
Tropical Islands (theme park), Germany **114**, 115
Turtles 53, **53**
Tyrannosaurus rex 72, **72**, 73

U
Uluru (Ayers Rock), Australia 24-25, **24-25**, 37
Upside-down house 118, **118**

V
Velociraptor 73
Virginia opossums 49, **49**
Volcanoes 18-19, **19**

W
Wandering albatrosses 67, **67**
Waterfalls **32**, 32-33, **33**, 123, **123**
Weddell seals 66, **66-67**
Wildebeests 56, **56**
Wingspans 67, 123, 124

Photo Credits

ASP: Alamy Stock Photo; DT: Dreamstime; GI: Getty Images; MP: Minden Pictures; NGIC: National Geographic Image Collection; SS: Shutterstock

All maps by NG Maps. Cover (UP RT), Ryan Benyi Photography ASP; (CTR RT), Denis Belitsky/SS; (LO RT), Shannon Alexander/SS; (LO CTR), Doug Meek/SS; (LO LE), QQ7/SS; (CTR LE), Brian C. Weed/SS; (UP LE), Sean Pavone/SS; (UP CTR), Banana Republic Images/SS; spine, Roman Sigaev/SS; back cover (LE), Jupiterimages/GI; (RT), turtix/SS; 1, Iakov Kalinin/Adobe Stock; 2-3, tawatchai1990/Adobe Stock; 4-5, Kseniya Ragozina/ASP; 10-11, Vietnam Stock Images/SS; 13 (UP), Coral Brunner/SS; 13 (LO), scubaluna/GI; 14-15, Altitude Visual/SS; 15, Andy Bardon/NGIC; 16 (UP), courtesy of NOAA Okeanos Explorer, Océano Profundo 2015; 16 (LO), courtesy of NOAA Office of Ocean Exploration and Research, 2016 Deepwater Exploration of the Marianas; 17, Emory Kristof And Alvin Chandler/NGIC; 19 (UP LE), Athit Perawongmetha/GI; 19 (UP RT), Robert Crow/SS; 19 (LO), Carsten Peter/NGIC; 20, Stephen Alvarez/NGIC; 21, Reinhard Dirscherl/ASP; 22-23 (BACKGROUND), Ian Trower/GI; 22, Ivan Kuzmin/Adobe Stock; 23 (UP LE), Dobermaraner/SS; 23 (UP RT), Guenter Fischer/GI; 23 (LO RT), Simon Shim/SS; 23 (LO LE), worldswildlifewonders/SS; 24-25, Ralph/Adobe Stock; 25, Oscity/SS; 26 (UP), Peter Steyn/ARDEA; 26 (LO), Kelly Falkner/National Science Foundation; 27 (LE), nito/SS; 27 (CTR LE), givaga/SS; 27 (CTR RT), Picsfive/SS; 27 (RT), Valentyn Volkov/SS; 28, Yegor Larin/SS; 29 (UP), Julian Schaldach/SS; 29 (LO RT), Anolis01/GI; 29 (LO LE), Chiyacat/SS; 30, Mike D Kock/Gallo Images/GI; 31, Victor Sotorilli Vieira/GI; 32, Alicenerr/DT; 33, Avigator-Photographer/GI; 34, Zhasminaivanova/DT; 35 (LE), Jamen Percy/DT; 35 (RT), james_stone76/SS; 36 (UP), Julian Schaldach/SS; 36 (LO RT), Chris Howey/SS; 36 (LO LE), DeltaOFF/SS; 37 (UP LE), Yongyut Kumsri/SS; 37 (UP RT), AvigatorPhotographer/GI; 37 (LO RT), Stanislav Fosenbauer/SS; 38-39, Peter Steyn/ARDEA; 40 (LE), Morkel Erasmus/GI; 40 (RT), WaterFrame/ASP; 41 (UP LE), hphimagelibrary/GI; 41 (UP RT), Fotos593/SS; 41 (CTR), GomezDavid/iStock; 41 (LO RT), Firepac/SS; 41 (LO LE), Alisdair Macdonald//SS; 42 (UP), Patrick K. Campbell/SS; 42 (LO), Mark Carwardine/SS; 43, Isselée/DT; 44-45, Doug Perrine/ASP; 44 (LO), Mike Hill/ASP; 45 (CTR LE), Constantinos Petrinos/MP; 45 (LO LE), Tui De Roy/MP; 46, FLPA/Gianpiero Ferrari/SS; 47 (UP LE), siridhata/SS; 47 (UP CTR), Anton Starikov/SS; 47 (UP RT), New Africa/SS; 47 (CTR RT), Newlight/DT; 47 (CTR CTR), Stratos Giannikos/SS; 47 (CTR LE), Spalnic/SS; 47 (LO), Hilary Andrews/NG Staff; 48, Eric Isselée/SS; 49 (UP LE), Mark Graf/ASP; 49 (UP RT), sandergroffen/GI; 49 (LO RT), Juergen Sohns/ASP; 49 (LO LE), Mark Chappell/age fotostock; 50-51, TDway/SS; 50, Sipa Asia/SS; 51, Hung_Chung_Chih/GI; 52, Starkov Roman/SS; 53 (UP), Adam Jones/GI; 53 (LO), marefoto/GI; 54, mandarchallawar/Adobe Stock; 55 (UP LE), Anna Azimi/SS; 55 (UP RT), Rohrlach/Adobe Stock; 55 (LO), Carmen Brown Photography/GI; 56, GJohnson2/iStock; 57 (UP), Belbaiz/SS; 57 (LO RT), joetsm/GI; 57 (LO LE), Auscape/GI; 59 (UP), Design Pics Inc/NGIC; 59 (LO), Medford Taylor/NGIC; 60, kali9/GI; 61 (UP LE), Sandra Vieira/EyeEm/GI; 61 (CTR RT), Eric Isselée/SS; 61 (LO RT), Oksana Kuzmina/ASP; 62, Elena Birkina/SS; 63 (LE), Ratana Prongjai/SS; 63 (LO), photofriday/SS; 63 (RT), sasimoto/SS; 64 (UP), jmmf/GI; 64 (CTR RT), 4FR/GI; 64 (LO), Jan Martin Will/SS; 65 (UP), EcoPrint/SS; 65 (LO LE), Oleg Senkov/SS; 65 (LO RT), Jurgen & Christine Sohns/GI; 66 (UP), Yva Momatiuk and John Eastcott/MP; 66 (LO), Frans Lanting/NGIC; 67 (UP), Jason Edwards/NGIC; 67 (LO), MZPHOTO.CZ/SS; 68, Eric Gevaert/SS; 69 (UP LE and UP RT), Thomas Marent/MP; 69 (LO), Jared Hobbs/ASP; 70-71 (LO), Mike Lane/FLPA/MP; 71 (UP LE), Thailand Wildlife/ASP; 71 (UP RT), Rohrlach/Adobe Stock; 72 (ALL), Franco Tempesta; 73 (UP LE and UP RT), Franco Tempesta; 73 (LO RT), Marques/SS; 73 (LO LE), Franco Tempesta; 74 (UP LE), FLPA/Gianpiero Ferrari/SS; 74 (UP RT), Mike Lane/FLPA/MP; 74 (LO RT), Patrick K. Campbell/SS; 74 (LO LE), Morkel Erasmus/GI; 75 (UP), Jared Hobbs/ASP; 75 (LO RT), Thomas Marent/MP; 75 (LO LE), Firepac/SS; 76-77, stevew_photo/Adobe Stock; 78, Smit/SS; 79 (UP), Africa Studio/SS; 79 (CTR LE), pikselstock/SS; 79 (eel), panda3800/SS; 79 (peas), MaraZe/SS; 79 (shrimp), akepong srichaichana/SS; 79 (bananas), Maks Narodenko/SS; 80 (LE), unpict/SS; 80 (UP RT), StockImageFactory/SS; 80 (LO), ordinary042/Adobe Stock; 81 (hot dog), Elkeflorida/DT; 81 (fries), Piksel/DT; 81 (taco), Hurst Photo/SS; 81 (chocolate), M. Unal Ozmen/SS; 81 (dumplings), szefei/SS; 81 (granola), Abramova Elena/SS; 82, EvgeniyBobrov/Adobe Stock; 83, Fine Art Images/Heritage Images/GI; 83 (LO), studiovin/SS; 84, LeoPatrizi/GI; 85 (UP), peshkov/Adobe Stock; 85 (LO), Anna Panova/SS; 86 (UP), Uwe Zänker/DT; 86 (LO), Imfoto/SS; 87, Jacek Chabraszewski/Adobe Stock; 88 (UP), Heike Brauer/SS; 88 (LO), D. Hurst/ASP; 89, KK Stock/SS; 90 (LE), Hurst Photo/SS; 90 (RT), hanif66/SS; 91 (UP LE), Chris Willson/ASP; 91 (UP RT), Axel Bueckert/SS; 91 (CTR RT), Photodisc; 91 (CTR), Metropolitan Museum of Art; 91 (LO LE), Nataliia Dvukhimenna/SS; 92-93, Matthew Corley/ASP; 93 (UP), Janice Storch/SS; 93 (LO), Ortis/SS; 94-95, Viorika/GI; 94 (LE), Rob Crandall/SS; 94 (RT), hidesy/SS; 95, Suzanne Long/ASP; 96 (chocolate), M. Unal Ozmen/SS; 96 (ice cream), unalozmen/GI; 96 (fries), Piksel/DT; 96 (pizza), images.etc/SS; 97 (dumplings), Jiang Hongyan/SS; 97 (hot dog), Elkeflorida/DT; 97 (taco), Hurst Photo/SS; 98-99, Tommy Alven/SS; 100, benedek/GI; 101 (UP), Franck Fotos/ASP; 101 (LO), Mardis/ASP; 102, Joseph Sohm/SS; 103 (LE), Francesco Dazzi/SS; 103 (RT), Bettmann/GI; 104-105, Piksel/DT; 104 (LE), Jim_Pintar/GI; 105 (UP RT), Sean Pavone/SS; 105 (LO LE), Marco Saracco/DT; 105 (LO RT), scaliger/GI; 106-107 (LO), aslysun/SS; 107 (UP), Shotshop GmbH/ASP; 107 (RT), tr3gin/SS; 108-109, Nataliia Budianska/SS; 109 (UP), Karl Johaentges/Look-foto/GI; 109 (LO), rusm/GI; 110, Pu Chao/Xinhua/GI; 111 (UP), Wiskerke/ASP; 111 (CTR RT), MACH Photos/SS; 111 (LO RT), Steve Speller/ASP; 111 (LO LE), TripDeeDee Photo/SS; 112 (LE), Granger.com - All rights reserved; 112 (RT), Chris Sattlberger/GI; 113 (UP), Chris Batson/ASP; 113 (LO LE), Carol Highsmith/Library of Congress Prints and Photographs Division; 113 (LO LE), Alizada Studios/SS; 114, Patrick Pleul/picture alliance via GI; 115 (UP), Graham Barclay/Bloomberg via GI; 115 (CTR RT), curved-light/ASP; 115 (LO), AP Photo/Kamran Jebreili; 116 (UP), Parinya Suwanitch/ASP; 116 (LO), Kurita KAKU/Gamma-Rapho via GI; 117 (UP), Julia700702/SS; 117 (LO), Michiel De Prins/ASP; 118, Stefan Sauer/picture alliance via Getty Image; 119, ronstik/Adobe Stock; 120 (UP LE), benedek/GI; 120 (UP RT), calvio/GI; 120 (LO RT), Mr Nai/SS; 120 (LO LE), Xinhua/Pu Chao via GI; 121 (UP), Aneese/SS; 121 (LO CTR), tr3gin/SS; 121 (LO LE), yulenochekk/GI; 121 (CTR LE), Typhoonski/DT; 122 (UP), ptashkan/Adobe Stock; 122 (LO), spass/Adobe Stock; 123 (LE), GlobalP/GI; 123 (RT), Paul Murtagh/SS; 124-125, Lunamarina/DT; 128, Fedor Selivanov/SS

FOR BRIA, WILL, LAWSON, BENNETT, AND LEO — JE

Published by Collins
An imprint of HarperCollins Publishers
1 Robroyston Gate,
Glasgow
G33 1JN
www.harpercollins.co.uk

HarperCollins Publishers
Macken House
39/40 Mayor Street Upper
Dublin 1
D01 C9W8
Ireland

© 2020 National Geographic Partners LLC. All rights reserved.
NATIONAL GEOGRAPHIC KIDS and Yellow Border Design are trademarks of National Geographic Society, used under license.

First published 2020
This edition 2026

ISBN 9780008825140

10 9 8 7 6 5 4 3 2 1

All rights reserved. No part of this publication may be reproduced, stored in a retrieval system, or transmitted, in any form or by any means, electronic, mechanical, photocopying, recording or otherwise without the prior permission in writing of the publisher and copyright owners.

Without limiting the exclusive rights of any author, contributor or the publisher of this publication, any unauthorised use of this publication to train generative artificial intelligence (AI) technologies is expressly prohibited. HarperCollins also exercise their rights under Article 4(3) of the Digital Single Market Directive 2019/790 and expressly reserve this publication from the text and data mining exception.

The contents of this publication are believed correct at the time of printing. Nevertheless the publisher can accept no responsibility for errors or omissions, changes in the detail given or for any expense or loss thereby caused.

HarperCollins does not warrant that any website mentioned in this title will be provided uninterrupted, that any website will be error free, that defects will be corrected, or that the website or the server that makes it available are free of viruses or bugs. For full terms and conditions please refer to the site terms provided on the website.

A catalogue record for this book is available from the British Library

Printed in India

If you would like to comment on any aspect of this book, please contact us at the above address or online.
natgeokidsbooks.co.uk
collins.reference@harpercollins.co.uk

The publisher would like to acknowledge and thank early childhood learning specialist Barbara Bradley for her expert insight and guidance. Many thanks also to project editor Erica J. Green, project manager Grace Hill Smith, and researcher Michelle Harris for their invaluable help with this book.